BOOTSTRAP LITERATURE:

preliterate societies do it themselves

Margaret M. Wendell
Summer Institute of Linguistics
Dallas, Texas

INTERNATIONAL READING ASSOCIATION
800 Barksdale Road   Newark, Delaware 19711

Copyright 1982 by the
International Reading Association, Inc.

Library of Congress Cataloging in Publication Data
Wendell, Margaret M., 1921-
  Bootstrap literature.

  Includes bibliographies.
  1. Authorship—Study and teaching. 2. New
literates, Writing for. 3. Literacy. I. Title.
PN181.W46   808'.02'07   81-11764
ISBN 0-87207-946-5   AACR2

Contents

ACKNOWLEDGEMENTS

Bookstrap Literature is a revision of my master's thesis, *Training Authors in a Preliterate Society,* completed in 1978 at the University of Texas at Arlington. Supervising professors Marvin K. Mayers, David H. Bendor-Samuel, and Virgil Poulter offered helpful criticism and advice, and then encouragement to try for wider circulation. I am grateful to them.

Dorothy Herzpg and Marjorie Buck were my principal colleagues in the 1970 workshop in Mexico where ideas contained in this book began to develop. Without their perceptive insight and desire to pursue new avenues the concept would have withered on the vine. Encouragement offered by Frank E. Robbins during that time is also deeply appreciated.

I am especially grateful to Margrit Bolli, Georgia Hunter, Frances Jackson, Mary Morgan, Isabel Murphy, and Frances Woods for their eagerness to share their own innovative ideas for training village writers.

Respondents to my questionnaire are too many to list, but their help was invaluable. Because they dropped other important work in order to send a reply in the next outgoing mail, I was able to get more recent data. And it was Nancy Straughan Lorenson who tracked my notations through the stack of letters to categorize and record the information, insisting all the while that it was a fun job.

At a low point in the writing—when barricades to clarity seemed hopeless to overcome—Victor and Riena Kondo flew in from South America. Despite a heavy travel and lecture schedule, Riena graciously gave scores of hours to reading the manuscript and offering suggestions for improvement. My gratitude for that timely help can never be adequately expressed.

The editing work of Faye Branca and her staff at the International Reading Association has been excellent, and I thank them.

At least five typists have willingly helped during various stages of the work. Margaret Gonzalez, typist of the final copy, exemplified them all with her painstaking attention to detail and personal interest in the book.

Above all, I want to acknowledge those men and women in both hemispheres, the indigenous writers themselves. They are working hard, many against great odds, to create something new and beautiful in their own languages, for their own societies. They have my deepest admiration and respect.

MMW

Foreword

Anthropologists for decades have reported to the literate world their observations of preliterate and neoliterate societies. More recently, readers in industrialized countries have been informed in books, magazines, and newspapers, viewers and listeners by television and radio, about the work of field linguists who encode, analyze, and classify the languages of minority groups. The massive efforts in this area are hastened and intensified for good reason. Many societies which have no written language and no way of keeping up with news essential to their welfare and safety are marked for early extinction, crowded out and pushed back and ridden with diseases. Should we do more for migratory birds? Should we lose the full evidence of verbal man's ingenuity and creative genius by stifling the native tongue in any society? While many linguists continue to map the world literacy, showing the tongues that unify or divide peoples regardless of national boundaries, illiteracy increases by population explosion, and disease and war have another chance to flare.

Historically, attempts to teach illiterate groups to read have failed (when they have failed) because the mother tongue is bypassed in favor of the national or regional tongue. Someone who tries to teach the second language as a first reading experience doubles the reader's hardship in memorization and, to a degree, loses the advantage of motivation which meaningful reading would provide. Furthermore, the mother tongue is the speaker's identity, which he needs for psychological and emotional security all his life (Laurens Van der Post).

The suggestion of this book by Margaret Wendell is that the habit of reading should be established in the reading of a newspaper in the mother tongue, with later editions in diglot. The wisdom of both ideas is considerable, as you will find.

How, in a six-week institute can students learn to write their own language and produce a newspaper which would be acceptable and interesting to the people in their village (including the chief), and impressive to neighboring groups who look down on illiterates? How can they afford to publish a paper worthy of respect, when large publishing companies charge more than they could ever pay? In their village it would be unthinkable to charge anything at all. Villagers freely share what they have.

As you see, the plot thickens. Without further delay, read on. Your respect for this book and the many people who contributed to it selflessly and circumspectly will more than equal the weight on your lap. Good reading! Better future!

Constance M. McCullough

Introduction

Many books have been produced on the subject of reading—how it is done, how it is taught, who teaches it, how it is learned and not learned, and how it relates to language and life. A topic which is *not* flooding the market concerns the reading problems of preliterate societies whose members speak one of some two thousand minority languages which either have no writing system, or which only recently have acquired a system to symbolize their thought or speech (Grimes, 1978).

In an age when libraries in major languages of the Western world are moving more and more into microprinting in order to house enormous masses of written material, it is astounding to discover that there are many small societies just now taking the first tentative step into literacy: writing the first page ever to exist in their own languages.

The gap between industrialized groups and these "forgotten people" is staggering to consider. How can a preliterate people possibly deal with societies that not only send men and vehicles into space and bring them back, but whose rural citizens have access to hundreds of pages of newsprint every day if they so choose? How can preliterate societies have any hope of survival in a world of such oceanwide disparity?

Unesco is one body that has long recognized that, in this fast-paced world, literacy is the major key to survival of a people or of a person. Many programs have been devised to remedy the problem of world illiteracy; some have been implemented. However, exploding population has outdistanced reading classes, and world statistics continue to show ever-increasing millions who cannot read or who do not read, despite stepped-up efforts to teach them.

Another concern of Unesco is the scarcity of books for developing countries, as is evidenced by its naming 1972 as International Book Year. Thus world attention began to focus on the fact that learning the skill of reading is one thing, but having enough materials to read and to establish the reading habit is quite another. Without progress toward the latter, the former is likely to be quickly lost, especially if the skill has been only half-acquired because it was presented through the mist of a second or third language.

In the past, relatively few large-scale literacy instruction programs have found it convenient to use the local minority languages as vehicles for reading or reading instruction. Reasons are many and primary among them are the lack of an alphabet, lack of pedagogical materials in local languages, lack of trained instructors, and lack of progressively difficult (graded) reading materials of sufficient quantity and calibre to set and sustain the reading process and to promote ease and interest in reading. Even where these elements may have been provided (as they were in certain cases), there are few instances where the production of an indigenous literature has consequently sprung up.

Bootstrap Literature is the description of a self-effort literature production process now gathering momentum in some 200 minority language groups located in both hemispheres. Speakers of these languages have been contacted by field linguists who act as "catalysts" or "facilitators" but not as "doers" in the process. Sponsored by the Summer Institute of Linguistics,* and working in agreement with governmental agencies of the respective countries, the field linguists lend their services in language analysis to initiate the selection of alphabets (or other symbolization as the situation may demand), and to encourage new readers and writers into an independent and ongoing production of reading materials

*The Summer Institute of Linguistics (SIL) is an international, nonprofit organization dedicated to scientific linguistic investigation of unwritten indigenous languages, and to literacy and Scripture translation in those languages. Sponsorship is by individuals and small local groups holding similar interests. For a complete description, see Brend and Pike, 1977.

which reflect the cultural interests and desires of the group. Thus mother tongue literature is authored by the local citizens themselves, not by the field linguist, and it is written in the language of the home. The content of the literature is that judged by the local authors to be of interest to their peers, whether for information or for entertainment.

It has become apparent that, through use of the materials the local authors produce, it is easier to 1) introduce the reading skill in linguistically isolated situations; 2) convey the notion that reading can become a relevant, meaningful, and exciting element in life (thus providing motivation to learn the skill); 3) provide several titles so that a variety of preferences as well as skill levels may be satisfied; and 4) set wheels in motion toward the goal of an ongoing process of literacy within a particular culture, without the continuing and pressuring presence of someone from outside that society.

What about "Progress"?

Obviously, it is unrealistic to assert that the ability to write one's own language is the cure-all for problems of attaining peace, progress, and prosperity. Nevertheless, the lack of skill in the area of written communication is a factor heavily involved in the social and economic imbalance of today's world.

For purposes of this book, primary focus will be upon the training of local writers as a means of enabling a preliterate, minority language group to make its own way, proudly, into twentieth century life to the degree which that society deems best, not as another group decides what is best for them.

Bootstrap literature can link the old with the new and the familiar with the foreign, providing opportunities for members of a preliterate or newly literate society to choose which way they might desire to go. Those whom others would "act upon" become not only the actors, but the directors of action for the enjoyment and benefit of their society.

What then is the role of consultants, the experts from outside? Their primary contribution is to help and encourage at the beginning, and to be willing to step out of the picture as speedily as possible. Careful planning must take place in order to accomplish these goals.

Informal reports of the results of such programs have indicated enough of a trend toward success that it now appears feasible to make a fuller presentation of the matter than has appeared to date (see Herzog, 1974; Van Dyken, 1977; Wendell, 1974, 1975).

In August 1977 a letter was sent to the literacy departents of all branches of the Summer Institute of Linguistics (SIL), as well as to individuals within the SIL context, who were known by the writer to have had experience in the area of training local authors. This letter was designed to extract information concerning the following points:

1. the extent of reading or understanding of the purpose of reading as noted in an indigenous group during initial contact by SIL personnel;
2. the situation of the group as it now stands, especially with regard to self-image and progress toward a state of literacy, or lack thereof;
3. the contribution of locally-authored materials to such change, if change is taking place;
4. the methods used in training writers;
5. the contribution of locally-authored materials to other aspects of linguistic investigation and the translation of other literature; and
6. the probability/improbability of development of an ongoing, indigenous literacy/literature program.

One hundred seventy-five letters were sent out, and eighty responses were received. Information from these replies, plus the writer's own experience and observations in the beginning phases of the program, are incorporated in the following chapters with the hope that they may prove helpful to other persons who are interested in literacy work and who may encounter similar challenges among preliterate peoples.

Overview of the Book

Part One of this book treats the rationale for training local writers—a way of introducing a preliterate society to the meaning, import, and pleasure of reading, and an eventual way of leading that same society into a self-sustaining state of literacy. Part Two deals with the specifics of the training process. It will hold interest for those who are actively involved or soon will be involved in organizing and presenting training in a workshop format.

Part One

Chapter 1 describes the early introduction of locally-authored literature into the life of a minority language group as a necessary step preceding a program to teach the skill of reading. Self-evaluation of the Unesco sponsored Experimental World Literacy Programme is cited, indicating that lack of such a step is one cause of failure in teaching reading in relation to local work or to the acquisition of a technological skill.

The development of indigenous writers as a major part of a literacy program involves the trainer, the community, and the trainee. These basic elements are set forth in Chapters 2 and 3. Examples of informal training, done on the local scene as chance opportunities present ideas for writing, are presented in Chater 4, supporting a strategy that may be preferable to formalized training. However, the more structured workshop-type training often presents to the trainees certain psychological advantages which may be lacking in a program held in the trainees' home environment.

Chapter 5 deals with the results to date as seen from the perspectives of the trainee, the indigenous society, the national educator, and the field linguist. Problem areas still to be resolved are pinpointed in Chapter 6. These lie principally in the areas of engaging community support and in establishing the concept as a part of community life. Difficulties concerning procurement of materials (paper, ink, and the like) are discussed, and challenge is given for innovation in tackling the problems.

Part Two

Chapter 7 describes decisions that must be made while planning a smooth-running workshop. Will a single language or several languages be represented? In what type of location should the workshop be held? Advance information, teaching personnel, and equipment are discussed in detail.

With the trainee in focus, Chapter 8 outlines and discusses classes and activities which are, of course, the backbone of a writer-training workshop.

Chapter 9 takes into account a specific and important section of the training—the discussion sessions held with the writer-trainees. Suggestions are given for the presentation of seventeen topics considered vital in the training.

Chapter 10 focuses on the sponsoring field linguist and his/her orientation to this aspect of the task. Twelve discussion topics are briefly outlined; background reading is suggested; and objectives and points for discussion are offered for each topic.

Chapter 11 briefly summarizes the viewpoint taken throughout the book. Supplementary materials and sample writings are found in the appendixes.

The author does not intend to imply that all that is to be said on the subject of indigenous writers has been said. Rather, it is hoped that inspiration may have been given for amplification, and for a sharing in writing of new insights and innovative procedures. Especially desired is a proposal for research that would statistically support or disprove the notion that to be most effective, literacy must have its beginnings within a society, and that its development must be largely self-propelled.

References

Brend, Ruth M., Pike, Kenneth L. *The Summer Institute of Linguistics: Its work and contributions*. The Hague: Mouton, 1977.

Grimes, Barbara F. (Ed.). *Ethnologue* (9th ed.). Huntington Beach, California: Wycliffe Bible Translators, 1978.

Herzog, Dorothy. A literature workshop: part I, part III, *Notes on Literacy*, 1974, *17*, 1-6; 16-22. (Reprinted in *Notes on literacy, selected articles*, 1979, 226-230; 241-246.)

Van Dyken, Julia. Towards readable writing. *Literacy Work*, 1977, *6*, 17-34.

Wendell, Margaret M. A literature workshop: part II. *Notes on Literacy*, 1974, *17*, 6-16. (Reprinted in *Notes on literacy, selected articles*, 1979, 231-240.)

Wendell, Margaret M. An experimental project for production of reading material in a preliterate society. *Notes on Literacy*, 1975, *18*, 1-9. (Reprinted in *Notes on literacy, selected articles*, 1979, 218-224.)

Wendell, Margaret M. Writer-training workshops. *Notes on Literacy*, 1975, *18*, 9-32. (Reprinted in *Notes on literacy, selected articles*, 1979, 251-267.)

Part One

Rationale for Training Indigenous Writers

Chapter One

World Literacy Programs and Preliterate Societies

[Arnold Toynbee] observed that mass education is a recent, and important invention. Since the eighteenth century, countries in the West have attempted to educate nearly everybody (Guthrie, 1978:64).

Innumerable programs to promote literacy in developing countries have been proposed by the Western World, and many programs have been implemented. Despite these efforts, reports by Unesco indicate that the total number of illiterates in the world continually increases even though the percentage decreases.* One reason for this discouraging fact is the rapid rate of increase in world population. But in this age of accelerated learning, why is it that reading—the very basis of formal education—is so difficult for the masses to acquire?

Is multiplicity of languages a significant factor in the failure of literacy programs? Have the minority languages been given sufficient consideration as programs were planned? Have divergent cultural aspects been taken into account as programs were applied? Have the programers studied the existing reading concepts, or has it been assumed that everyone has the same basic understanding that the purpose of the printed page is communication? Have current attitudes toward minority languages (as held by speakers of dominant lan-

*In 1978, the world's illiterates totaled more than 800 million according to Unesco's Julian Behrstock in his address to the Seventh International Reading Association World Congress on Reading in Hamburg, Germany (Behrstock, 1980:316).

guages, by minority language speakers themselves, and by the programers or their agents) been studied as vital effective components of a proposed program? Most important, has a worthwhile literature been made available, fostering a reading habit?

Questions such as these concerning minority languages and cultures, writing as communication, and sociolinguistic factors can help to pinpoint reasons for failure and provide general guidelines for success.

As noted previously, literacy programs abound. Some are sponsored by private groups from the industrialized nations, and some are sponsored jointly by representatives of the industrialized world and by the government of the host country. The most ambitious of recent efforts is the Experimental World Literacy Programme (EWLP) sponsored jointly by Unesco and the governments of the eleven nations involved. This program merits some description and comment because of its official nature, involving governments of several countries; because of its worldwide scale; and because its assumptons are typical of those held by most literacy organizations. It is in the area of assumptions that contrast is found with the point of view expressed in this chapter.

The strategy employed by EWLP links literacy with economic development, i.e., the teaching of the reading process by using material based on the learning of a technological skill which will enhance the learner's opportunity for employment. It is expected that, ultimately, the entire nation will benefit economically.

After ten years of program experimentation in eleven countries involving thousands of people and at least 32 million dollars, a comprehensive and frank evaluation was published: *The Experimental World Literacy Programme: A Critical Assessment* (1976). While some measure of success can be counted, the report indicates that such a program is far from being the answer to what is now judged to be a highly complex problem.

Donald F. Solá's 1966 assessment of the EWLP in its beginning stages pointed out that Unesco's failure to include specialists in linguistics and sociology would seriously affect the efficacy of the program in its outworking. The evaluation on subsequent events proved Solá's criticism valid.

Unesco's analysis of the EWLP reveals that, of a wide variety of problems, language was among the foremost (Unesco, 1976:168-170). The multiplicity and diversity of languages within a given country presented unforeseen problems such as the difficulty of communication through translated materials, thereby creating a complexity of sociological problems which deeply affected the target groups.

The translation of information concerning technological skills often had to be conveyed through the medium of two or three languages. For example, explanation of procedures based on technological skills originally developed by Russians had to be translated from Russian into English and then into the national language, after which it was taught to learners (of reading, not of language) who did not speak any one of the three languages (p. 169).

The accuracy of the translations was highly suspect both as representing the meaning of the original, and as to intelligibility in the target language. It is even more important to consider the confusion that even an accurate presentation could create in the mind of the beleaguered student who is required to learn simultaneously, not one but three new elements: a new language skill, a new technological skill, and a reading skill based upon the two preceding "unknowns." It is no wonder the evaluators discovered a student dropout rate that soared as high as 95 percent in areas where a minority language and nonurban lifestyles were predominant (p. 162).

Furthermore, the evaluators point out that failure to learn to read was not the only problem—nor even the major problem. Of far deeper import, with long-lasting effect upon the lives of the learners, was the imposition of a national language upon people from a minority language group. They subsequently suffered increased "feelings of inferiority and repression" rather than self-realization leading to the liberation of spirit which was, along with technological advancement, the intended goal. By ignoring the local language (principally because no one knew how to write it), and by insisting upon the use of the national language (because of economics of publishing as well as mastery by program agents), directors unwittingly provided indisputable and tangible proof to the learners that their local language could not serve for written communication and, therefore, was of no value.

Lloyd W. Kline has well expressed the significance of the problem: "My language is my own. To speak to me in your tongue, which is not my own, and expect me to follow what you say is to put my language down, exalt your own, and denigrate me a bit in the process" (Kline, 1978: 199).

Successful teaching demands two basic elements: consideration of what the pupil already knows and clear communication of the new subject, building upon the previous knowledge. With regard to successful instigation of change (which in a sense involves a teaching process), Dell Hymes has summed up current thought: ". . . in order to bring about change, one must first accept people for what and who they are" (see Heath, 1972: Preface, ix). Language is inextricably bound into "what and who" a person is, and must be honored in any type of successful teaching or instigation of change. Communication must be clear, involving the language the pupil knows.

We can quickly see that neither basic teaching elements, nor the core element of a successful change program, i.e., acceptance of the learners, entered into the above cited example. The materials to teach reading were related, in content, to two new elements: a new language and a new technology. Clear communication, in the language of the worker, did not take place. By exclusive use of the national language, the program exhibited no respect for what the learners represented as members of a minority language group. The resultant failure to learn, brought about by such omissions, can affect the whole society as well as the individuals involved. Instead of bringing desired change—from illiteracy to literacy—a deeper entrenchment is made of the group's convictions that 1) reading is beyond the capabilities of minority language speakers and 2) they are the social, economic, and linguistic underdogs.

While the purpose of the EWLP is highly practical and could make a significant contribution toward the desired goal of worldwide literacy, it should be recognized that its usefulness lies primarily among illiterate people who speak major languages which already have a history of reading and writing. The usefulness of its strategy among linguistic minorities, especially those of preliterate societies, is very doubtful. (*Preliterate* is defined by Webster, 1976, as "not yet employing writing as a cultural medium.")

That reading activity should be relevant to life's activity is a sound principle, one with which any educator is in agreement. It is in the EWLP definition of "life's activity" that inadequacy is found. Such activity should be seen as that which is *within* a particular culture, and that which lies next to the heart of the people of its society. This activity may or may not be work-related. It is inadequate to relate "life's activity" only to the domain of change or development, implying new technologies, new skills, new concepts. Furthermore, the deeply embedded Western notion that the ultimate purpose of literacy is primarily to increase accumulation of material goods is not necessarily shared by other cultures. Literacy may offer other benefits of a deeper and longer-lasting nature.*

The appendix to the Unesco report includes several pages of recommendations concerning further implementation of a work-related program: ". . . the concept of functionality must be extended to include all its dimensions: political, economic, social, and cultural" (p.191). It is briefly acknowledged that to begin literacy in the mother tongue is the preferred procedure, with a recommendation that thee be "linguistic research . . . to improve the efficiency of literacy (dictionaries, vocabularies, grammars, literature for new literates)" (pp. 192-193). The evaluators state that such an aim raises problems such as "untranscribed languages, lack of instructors and books, costs, etc." No suggestion is made as to how these could be handled other than that they *be* handled.

Also noted among the recommendations is the desirability of encouraging "individuals and groups to express themselves orally, in writing or in other ways . . . illiterate adults must not be mere receivers of knowledge, but also creators of culture." Such production is an essential part of a sound literacy program, deserving at least as much attention as that given to the recommended resource materials: ". . . manuals, practical guides, bibliographies and teaching documents" (p. 193).

What suggestions might be made for making literacy both relevant and functional for preliterate societies? A

---

*Interestingly, only 28 percent of Americans, surveyed as to reasons why they read, chose Upgrading of Work Skills as a purpose. More frequently chosen were: General Knowledge, 69 percent; Recreation, 56 percent; and Relaxation, 41 percent (Guthrie, 1979:752).

broader-based program with in-depth attention to the language, the culture, and to sociological demands is strongly urged. Such a program would include three main elements: 1) intensive linguistic study culminating in a tentative orthographic system appropriate to the linguistic and sociocultural factors involved; 2) training local citizens to create a beginning literature by writing their own thoughts and experiences in the local cultural and linguistic framework; and 3) teaching the skill of reading in the local language to the larger community, with transfer to both speaking and reading knowledge of the national or dominant language as the group itself deems necessary.

The purpose of the present study is to examine in detail the second feature, training of local authors. Some of the examples to be cited in this study will reveal a helpful relationship of author training to the problem of choosing a satisfactory orthography. It will also be seen that writer training can awaken interest in reading and in the teaching of reading within the local group. Furthermore, local authors can be the key to enable a minority group to unlock doors to a second language and culture, the understanding of which may be of vital importance to them.

Of primary importance, the training of local authors can promote a continuing flow of reading material relevant in the local context. Without this prospect of literature production to stimulate, encourage, and establish the reading habit, new literates will quickly fall back into illiteracy. A survey conducted by J. A. Abhari, concerning the publication of easy-to-read materials for new literates, states that the lack thereof is probably the most important reason for failure of adult literacy programs. Of eight villages in Iran, surveyed to determine the measure of success of previous literacy efforts, only one was found to have continuing readers. It was in this village alone that a library and publications stand were found. "The semiliterates in this village read more often, spent more money on reading materials, and scored highest in a test which was administered to measure literacy skills" (Abhari, 1978:176).

It is quickly acknowledged that successful author training with production of good materials does not imply a simple process that can be accomplished in a matter of weeks or even months. Depending on the situation and the current motivation of the preliterate group, it could take many years. However, the materials produced by local authors should give the society in focus a sound, basic understanding of the nature and purpose of the printed page without which linguistic minority groups are unlikely to gain anything more than a thin veneer of literacy, no matter how intensive the program to teach the skill of reading.

Concepts of Reading

Literacy teachers, fresh from a literate world, often fail to recognize that a preliterate people already may have formed a mental concept of reading that drastically differs from their own. Newcomers often instigate their programs, thinking they operate on the basis of mutual understanding that reading is a form of communication. Investigation, however, has shown that there may be a completely divergent viewpoint. The following examples reveal that reading means many things for many preliterate people, but seldom does it mean communication.

Reading Means Prestige

In Latin America, it has been found that many indigenous groups consider reading has but one purpose: to learn a second and prestigious language, such as Spanish or Portuguese. An example typifying such belief comes from one of the Otomí (Mexico) groups where Otomí speakers look in bewilderment at a booklet written in their language and ask, "Why should we read Otomí? We already *know* Otomí!" Underlying these words is the age-old realization that unless they learn to speak the national language, their chances of being considered "whole persons" are slim.

A current study of four Navajo students' concept of reading revealed that they, too, associate the reading process with language learning. They indicated that its specific purpose is to enable the reader to produce acceptable English grammar (DuBois, 1979:691).

Other groups equate reading directly with the acquisition of prestige. Some investigators have reported requests for a medicine that will enable the recipient to read and thus to be known as an educated person.

A Piro woman of Peru was observed by an SIL field linguist to be fully absorbed in reading, as she sat on a low bench in the linguist's house. After an hour or more, the field linguist could no longer restrain her curiosity as to what this fascinating piece of literature could be, so she drew nearer the reader. To her amazement, the book, held upside down, was one of her own linguistic journals which the woman had doubtless seen her "model" studying on a previous occasion. Whether the immediate objective was prestige or whether the woman had some other motive in mind, is not known. In any case, there was belief that holding the book and gazing at it intently would surely bring some kind of benefit.

Reading Means Christianity

Reports indicate that indigenous groups often make a strong connection between reading and conversion to Christianity, sometimes with individuals commenting that they could never become Christians since they do not know how to read. In their experience, Christians are the only ones seen with books in their hands. Cause and effect have thus become reversed in the observers' eyes.

Some who have already embraced Christianity are of the opinion that the ability to read will automatically produce a sinless life. Great is the disillusionment and perplexity when observation and experience disprove their theory.

All Books Are Holy Literature

Still others of the indigenous Christian sector have responded to *all* reading material with the awe reserved for "Holy Writ," since their reading experience has been centered almost exclusively on Scripture or hymns. In one group, a booklet concerning a new agricultural method, which the older men of a community had helped to plan and to phrase, took on this same "holy" aspect once it appeared in written form. When the agriculturist found that certain parts needed revision, the elders objected to any change being made in the text on the grounds of the honored place the agriculture booklet now occupied among the sacred writings.

Books Are Anticipated Meaninglessness

Many indigenous people of Latin America, speaking primarily their own language, have attended school conducted totally in Spanish and some have mastered the system of calling the correct sounds in response to the symbols they see on the page of the textbook. To many of this group, the objective of fluent reading is to race through a given passage as rapidly and as loudly as possible, ignoring all pause indicators. When asked to explain what has just been read, the reader may respond indignantly, "You asked me to read that, and I did. Now don't ask for something completely irrelevant." Unless much time and effort are expended in learning to *speak* the dominant language, learning to read it probably does more harm than good since learners miss the point that reading is a form of communication. In fact, what they learn is that reading has nothing at all to do with communication; it is sound-calling and nothing more.

In Latin America, sound-calling as a substitute for reading has its roots in the centuries-old practice of using an unfamiliar language, Spanish or Portuguese, as a vehicle for teaching. In Nepal, the same result has been noted among the rural Dhangur Kurux people who learned to read *in their own language*. Because the reading material was couched in an elevated literary style developed centuries before, the Dhangur Kurux of today are unable to comprehend its meaning. The report states:

> [They are expected] only to repeat the [lesson material] verbatim, matching graphic form with correct pronunciation. In general, they are not asked to explain the meaning of what is read. Moreover, had they wished to understand it (which, in general, they are programed not to), they would have difficulty, for in most cases . . . the materials used for teaching reading contain words and phrases and a literary style that are completely unrelated to their experiences of the world (Gordon, 1978).

Reading Is Defined by Observable Behavior

In many indigenous languages, the word for "read" has the literal meaning of "look-at-paper." In at least one language of Mexico, the inherent meaning is even more exact: "talk-to-paper." The Gahuku people of Papua New Guinea use the expression "to-count-the-carvings." Reasons for these three expressions can be understood easily when one pictures a silent reader, an oral reader using a language foreign to the observer, and a slow reader who points to each word with a finger when reading aloud.

Books Are Desirable for Paper

In the highlands of Papua New Guinea, some groups have been found to welcome the introduction of primers and pamphlets, for the booklets provide coveted material in which to roll the locally grown tobacco into cigarettes. The pages also may serve as fresh material for decorative armbands.

Books Provide a Key to Treasure

The "cargo cult" culture of Papua New Guinea teaches that reading is the white person's "key" for claiming the ancestral treasures originally intended for Papuans. Incentive for capturing the key is therefore high at the beginning of a literacy program, but can be rapidly lost when the reading is found to produce no immediate treasure.

All Paper Is Money

Having seen white people first hand pieces of paper to a seller of goods, then pick up the items chosen and walk away, Cuiba people of Colombia quite naturally assumed that all paper would be equally useful. When they discovered that it was not, they simply concluded that paper was just another tool of the white person's inscrutable world. It certainly had no place or meaning in theirs. (It took six years of firsthand observation of two field linguists' daily use of paper and pencil before the first glimmer of interest was displayed by the Cuibas.)

Such basic misconceptions of either the reading process or the purpose of reading illustrate the futility of superimposing another system, in another language, upon a people who are cognitively unprepared to receive and interpret that system. Risk is taken even in the use of minority language when the lesson content is based only on a translation of concepts from an industrialized society. There must be common ground between the teacher and the learner before effective teaching and learning can take place, and the responsibility for discovery of that ground rests upon the teacher.

Attitudes toward Language

Another factor affecting the psychological readiness of the group for learning to read lies in the area of attitude toward the minority language as compared with attitude toward the dominant language. The way the minority language is regarded by speakers of the dominant language, by the educator or other agent of change, and by the minority language speakers themselves, can seriously affect the outcome of a basic literacy program. These attitudes must be studied and taken into account at the outset of any program, for they can either effectively stimulate or greatly hinder a literacy program.

Attitudes of Major Language Speakers

In the Western Hemisphere, the history of linguistic conflict between colonists and indigenous people is long and, for the most part, bitter. In the early days of the conquest of Mexico, certain priest-educators instituted Indian schools, teaching sons of the conquered Aztec nobles to read and write in Latin. Some priests learned the Nahuatl language and expanded the instruction to include writing in that language. Their students quickly caught on to the system and began writing their own histories, utilizing the orthographies designed by the priest-linguists. Such activity spelled political danger and eventually brought legislation by the conquerors which forbade use of any Indian language in school activity.

The new laws effectively squelched the formal learning processes and also created certain myths concerning language which persist to the present. Statements such as "What the Totonacs speak is not a language because it has no grammar and no written literature" have been heard frequently among the middle-class Latins. Happily, current efforts of Mexican educators and community development leaders are directed toward changing such ideas. This particular myth is not confined to Mexico.

Fishman (1972b:20) states that "the availability of dictionaries and grammars is taken as a sure sign that a particular variety (of language) is 'really a language.'" Apparently the notion is universal that a language *is* a language only when such elements are found. Statements of like nature, as ridiculous as they may sound, are often repeated by the middle social classes in most of the Latin American countries. This is not true at the university level where there is a completely realistic view of the indigenous languages, brought about as the study of anthropology and linguistics has become more popular.

Some countries acknowledge the usefulness of their indigenous languages to the extent of using them as vehicles to introduce reading at the first grade level in school. Thus the minority language is held as a bridge into education in the dominant language. Presumably, once students have arrived on the other side, i.e., speak the dominant language, they are expected to burn the bridge. With one notable exception, no country has made provision nor given encouragement to speakers of the dominant langauge to step onto the bridge and cross over to the side of the indigenous people. That exception is Peru, which recently became a leader among the American countries, if not the world, in correcting the one-sided approach to language and education. The Peruvian indigenous languages were declared to be official national languages, of equal value and usefulness, even in court (Ley General de Educación, 1972). Monolingual Spanish speaking students are required to learn at least one of the indigenous languages, some of which are taught in accredited courses in the universities.

It is encouraging that after some four hundred years, at least one country is taking steps to remedy a centuries-old sociolinguistic situation which has brought despair and needless feelings of gross inferiority to speakers of socially unacceptable languages.

Dictionaries and grammars are gradually appearing in many of the minority languages, compiled and published mainly by scholars from the Western world. But a written literature? Self-sustained literacy? Such continue to be the missing elements of the culture of minority language groups, elements urgently needed if the minorities are to consider themselves on a par with the dominant society, and if the dominant society is to exhibit the understanding and respect the minority languages deserve.

Attitudes of Educators
The attitudes educators have toward minority language speakers depend in part upon their own linguistic orientation and background, and even more upon the desires and goals of their sponsoring organizations which may be heavily influenced in their programing by the exigencies of time and

funds. It is rare that either the sponsoring group or their representative understands experientially the situation to be faced. The evaluators of EWLP noted that

> The present generation of specialists in industrialized countries—who were expected to provide much of the expertise for designing, implementing, and assessing EWLP—simply does not have personal experience of literacy as a chronic national problem (Unesco, 1976:11).

In this regard, Goodenough (1963) speaks of the necessity for "cultural empathy" on the part of the change agent. This is difficult to develop. It is especially difficult to understand just what it means to live and operate within a preliterate society, when all one's previous experience has been in a basically literate society.

Unless the educator is fully aware of the sociological and psychological problems besetting the minority group because its language has occupied an inferior position historically, it is all too easy to decide to use the national language as the mode for a literacy program. Furthermore, unless educators have facility in acquiring a speaking ability in the local language, they are all the more prone to opt for the national language as the vehicle for instruction. And unless there is keen awareness that the single, basic teaching principle of proceeding from the known to the unknown has its beginning in *language*, the educator might well choose to teach reading in the national language, considering that to be the most direct method and, therefore, the fastest way to reach the goal. Even though reason may indicate that reading in the vernacular will provide the most meaning for the learners and is the place to begin, lack of available materials in the local language can be a strong factor in a decision to go the route of the major language as the vehicle for teaching reading. It is rare to find educators who are convinced of the feasibility of using an indigenous language, unless they have had extensive linguistic training.

A number of years ago I had contact with a private European foundation which had as its objective the promotion of community development, including literacy, in African countries by means of televised teaching. It was revealed that in Ghana the programing was presented entirely in English.

When the director of the TV project was asked about provision being made for teaching monolingual illiterate speakers of the various Ghanaian languages, the reply was made: "The dialects cannot be learned, and they certainly cannot be written. Everything has to be in English." The director's flat refusal even to consider the problem of comprehension encountered by minority language speakers showed not only a lack of preparation for using the local languages in accomplishing the objectives, but also his attitude toward them.

Attitudes of Minority Language Speakers

Fishman has said that a person's language is a manifestation not just of thought, but of the very soul (1972a:46). What touches the heart more than praise of one's language, or way of expression? Conversely, what wounds the innermost being more deeply than ridicule of one's language or accent? Language and soul, or speech and personality, are so intertwined that when one is applauded, the other glows. Or when one is despised, the other despairs.

One's conscious attitude toward one's language—and then toward oneself—depends largely upon how others think about that person's language and how it is valued. In countries such as the United States and those of Latin America, there is a long history of social domination of a European language over the indigenous languages. Indigenous people may, in their innermost beings, love their language for its beauty and depth of expression, but at the same time be forced to conclude that it is worthless as they discover its inadequacy for social contact with the rest of the world. Thus they learn to disdain their language, and in so doing, to despise themselves. It is little wonder that people of indigenous origin, upon taking up residence in an urban center where the dominant language is used exclusively, will often vigorously deny knowing or speaking an indigenous language. They thus reject their language, and in so doing, albeit unconsciously, reject themselves.

In other areas of the world, such as in West Africa, the picture is somewhat distinct. Everyone in Ghana, for example, speaks a minority language, from the chief magistrate on down the economic and social ladder to the lowest rung. Nevertheless, it is recognized that the national language, English, is the one by which one moves in any area beyond the local community. A gentleman from the Vagla group expressed it thus: "If you go to a city such as Tamale, and you can't speak English, you look and feel like a fool! You can't find your way around, you can't ask directions, you can't even buy food, and the people laugh at you." While such experiences do not necessarily destroy one's confidence in one's mother tongue, the inability to rely upon one's own language, in one's own country, is most keenly felt.

Despite these pressures from without and from within, one of the most striking observations of the early writer-training efforts sponsored by the Summer Institute of Linguistics was the enthusiastic response of trainees 1) when they fully understood that the writing was to be entirely "theirs," i.e., in their own style as well as language, and on whatever topic they chose to write and 2) when their efforts were sincerely appreciated and applauded by speakers of the national language. These positive reactions were so strong that even the instructors who had predicted them were astonished.

Summary

The Experimental World Literacy Program (EWLP), cosponsored by Unesco and governments of developing countries, has been cited as the most recent and prestigious of world literacy programs whose aim is to reduce the rate of illiteracy in developing nations.

The Unesco sponsored evaluators of EWLP have noted that the strategy for teaching reading (i.e., with lessons based on instruction of a new technology and with the goal of economic betterment) has had little success in areas occupied by indigenous groups whose languages have no writing systems. Reasons for such failure are given as disregard for the linguistic, social, and cognitive systems; disregard for sensible teaching strategy involving known linguistic and cultural elements; and disregard for sociological problems brought on by further imposition of dominant language and culture norms upon a society already convinced of its inferior position.

World literacy program designers tend to assume that everyone in the world is eager to learn to read in order to improve his/her economic lot in life. While economic improvement is a deeply embedded motivation in industrialized societies, it must not be assumed that every society holds that same value nor that literacy brings immediate attainment of wealth. Another underlying assumption of programs such as the EWLP is that there is universal understanding of the nature and purpose of reading, i.e., that it is a form of communication. Examples from many indigenous groups show that such an assumption is not valid; the experience of many preliterate people with the printed page has led to great confusion concerning the real nature and purpose of reading.

EWLP evaluators suggested, among other things, that local authors be encouraged to write within their own cultural and linguistic framework. This is a worthy goal and should be given a prominent place in planning. We have pointed out, however, that promotion of such activity is difficult under the existing psychological blanket of negative attitudes toward the minority languages and their speakers.

Such negative attitudes are exhibited by 1) speakers of the dominant languages, usually because of a history of conflict between dominant and minority cultures; 2) educators who reflect their own and their sponsors' linguistic prejudices and experiential naivete; and 3) the minority language groups themselves who may reflect the attitudes of the other two entities to such a degree that the speakers likewise denigrate their own languages, and thus despise themselves.

It is obvious that before indigenous persons, speaking a minority language in a preliterate society, can enter fully into the world of literacy, something must convince them that reading is a vital means of communication and that they too, can enter into the world of books through the context of their own language and culture, and enjoy the process thoroughly.

References

Abhari, J.A. Easy to read materials for adult semiliterates: An international survey. In Dina Feitelson (Ed.), *Cross-cultural perspectives on reading and reading research.* Newark, Delaware: International Reading Assocition, 1978.

Behrstock, Julian. Books for all: International cooperation to promote reading. *Journal of Reading,* 1980, *23,* 313-319.

DuBois, Diane. Getting meaning from print: Four Navajo students. *Reading Teacher,* 1979, *32,* 691-695.

Fishman, Joshua. *Language and nationalism: Two integrative essays.* Rowley, Massachusetts: Newbury House, 1972(a).

Fishman, Joshua. *The sociology of language.* Rowley, Massachusetts: Newbury House, 1972(b).

Goodenough, Ward Hunt. *Cooperation in change.* New York: Russell Sage Foundation, 1963.

Gordon, Kent. Personal communication. Dallas, Texas: Summer Institute of Linguistics.

Guthrie, John T. Remembering content. *Journal of Reading,* 1978, *22,* 64-66.

Guthrie, John T. Why people (say they) read. *Reading Teacher,* 1979, *32,* 752-755.

Heath, Shirley Brice. *Telling tongues.* New York: Teachers College Press, 1972.

Kline, Lloyd W. That which is lost in translation. In Dina Feitelson (Ed.), *Cross-cultural perspectives on reading and reading research.* Newark, Delaware: International Reading Association, 1978.

Ley General de Educación. Decreto Ley No. 19326. Lima, Peru: Ministerio de Educación, 1972.

Solá, Donald F. *The U.N. experimental world literacy programme.* mimeographed paper, 1966.

Unesco. *The experimental world literacy programme: A critical assessment.* Paris: Unesco, 1976.

Chapter Two

Initial Steps to Provide Meaningful Literature

Individual Effort

For a number of years, some members of the Summer Institute of Linguistics have developed easy reading materials on an informal basis in the communities where linguistic studies were being done. They have been alert to turn seemingly minor incidents of the daily scene into interesting written material.

Martha Duff (1966) recounts how, in the early stages of linguistic analysis of the Amuesha language of Peru, she obtained the first entry for the future "Amuesha Library Series." Her coworker had just brought a pail of water from the nearby stream and before taking it into the house had flipped out a tiny minnow which had inadvertently been dipped up in the bucket. The fish was subsequently rescued by being placed in glass of water. Observing the incident, the Amuesha language teacher began to tell a first person experience story. Speaking as if she were the minnow, she described how "she" had been rescued from death by being placed in water. "There I breathed again. My heart got good again." The story was intended to be nothing more than a time-filler in a day of employment as a language teacher. However, the "pupil" was quick to recognize that this could serve three purposes: 1) her own language learning experience, 2) an amusing story that could be easily read by future new literates, and 3) an opportunity for the language teacher to see herself as an author.

After the minnow was returned to the stream, the teacher was asked to retell the story now including the minnow's reaction to its return home; the story with its new ending was then recorded in writing. Later it was made into a pamphlet and used as one small item out of many items for easy reading material for new literates.

Field linguists, in the throes of learning a hitherto unwritten language, are accustomed to making use of all kinds of incidents related orally by village people as a help in linguistic analysis and language learning. However, they are not always conscious of the need to take one more step and make the same material usable for reading purposes in the community. It takes very little effort to extend the usefulness of such material, perhaps only an extra carbon copy. The next step is to get that copy into someone's hands—perhaps the storyteller's, since that person is the most intimately involved.

Much can be done on an informal, individual level to contribute to the creation of a written language in a preliterate society, without formal training programs. The reward for a brief expenditure of time and effort can be handsome, either in awakening interest in writing or in establishing a realistic psychological relationship between oral speech and written speech or both.

Interestingly, most educators or other agents of change assume that to catch the interest of preliterate people, the content of a written piece must be something new to the hearer/reader. But it is seldom true that preliterate people are, in fact, so longing to find out about all the marvels of the rest of the world that they will go through the tedious process of learning to read. One of the best examples in defense of the theory that what is really most interesting is that which is most familiar comes from Colombia, South America:

> . . . one particular linguistic team . . . obtained from their language helper a list of the wild animals found in the area. Then they asked him to sit down beside the tape recorder and tell into the microphone all he could think of about these animals. After a few minutes of practice, the language helper was able to record, easily and naturally, such facts as the color and size of the animal, how it bears and takes care of its young, what it eats, whether or not it can be eaten, and whether or not it is dangerous to man.
>
> One of the linguists then transcribed these descriptions, none of which was very long, drew pictures to illustrate them, being very careful to check frequently with the [author] to see that they were more or less accurate, and typed it all up in a booklet form.

The reaction of the illiterate language helper, as he watched the book grow, was a very strong one. He touched the book, almost with awe, and said, "It is beautiful." Then he turned to the linguists, and with desire hitherto unseen, demanded, "When are you going to teach me to read?" (Wendell, 1975:3-4).

From a much more sophisticated Camerounian society came a report bearing the same impact concerning familiarity. The Ejagam people (largely literate in English) were skeptical of the value of books in their language, since they could see no immediate relationship to their goal of "passing school examinations in English." But once they caught sight of a book of Ejagam folktales which one of their number had been persuaded to write, they eagerly bought out the edition and demanded more.

Writer training among preliterate people closely parallels writing activity taught in some American schools to first and second grade school children, along with or even preceding reading instruction. Sealey, Sealey, and Millmore (1979:2) state that children in early grades are often attracted to writing as a form of self-expression

... just because it is new .... But making a start is not enough; it is essential that children go on to become writers in the sense that they turn naturally to that mode of expression when it seems appropriate. The inculcation of this attitude is a much harder task.

Perseverance in conditioning such attitudes reaps good results, whether among American school children or among adults of preliterate societies of Papua New Guinea or wherever. When the results are readers who are more attracted to materials produced by their peers than they are to colorful magazines such as the *National Geographic*, educators may know that their efforts have paid off. Interest of this intensity has been reported, but only when the field linguists were willing to spend time during early stages of their language investigation to encourage their language teachers and others to become aware of producing their own written material.

How can preliterates become creative writers if they cannot read or form letters to spell words? At this stage of literacy, the most commonly used tool in both the modern school and the remote jungle village is the tape recorder, with subsequent transcription of the material into booklet form by the teacher or field linguist (Sealey et al., p. 15). Also, in many of today's developing societies there are those who have had some schooling in a national or dominant language and who have learned to read and write in that language, to some degree of proficiency. Maybe the early materials will find a beginning with these people. In some cases, it has been discovered that even semiliterate persons long have had an overwhelming desire to express themselves in their own language but have not known how to begin. The field linguist has merely had to give early guidance and encouragement, and the writer was off and running.

First Formalized Effort

In March 1970 the Mexico Branch of the Summer Institute of Linguistics held its first indigenous writer training workshop. Writer training was not the intended focus of the course when it was scheduled a year earlier. The stated purpose at that time was the production of "easy reading material," since the need for such had long been recognized. Experience had shown that students who completed a primer did not automatically become full-blown readers. Previous efforts to produce easy to read literature had concentrated mainly on productions such as health books, how-to-do-its, translated stories of national heroes, and dictionaries or small vocabularies with vernacular-Spanish, and Spanish-vernacular entries. Content of the narratives had heavy emphasis upon the world beyond the confines of the indigenous people. Gradually, it had been recognized that content itself would have to change and would have to be pertinent and innately attractive to the local ethnic group. Authorship, however, was still tacitly considered to be the responsibility of the field linguist.

Unesco has advocated a minimum of 800 pages of supplementary reading material as that which is necessary to take a learner from the primer stage to independent reading. The task therefore of providing statisfactory reading material in sufficient variety to help a whole society to become literate had loomed as an overwhelming burden upon the SIL members involved in a heavy program of linguistic study and Scripture translation. It was only natural that some demanded the assistance of a second team, or that they chose to ignore the matter of supplementary reading material, hoping the problem would either miraculously resolve itself or go away automatically with the increase of schools in the national language.

The 1970 workshop marked a beginning in the change of perspective and offered brighter prospects for meeting the need of graded (i.e., easy-to-difficult) reading material. But the most exciting aspect of this course was that it opened possibilities for truly indigenous, ongoing literacy programs that could eventually help these societies become literate in their own languages.

Ten native speakers of eight different indigenous languages participated in the 1970 workshop held at an SIL study center located about 100 miles north of Mexico City. A few participants were monolingual speakers of their language, others were more or less proficient in Spanish as well as in their mother tongue. Educational backgrounds varied. Some had no schooling whatsoever, while others had completed primary school. (For fuller details, see Herzog, 1974 and Wendell, 1974.)

The objective of the workshop was to produce graded reading material, beginning with that which would be easiest for the new literate to read. The first problem, therefore, was to define the elements that make up easy reading material, the content of which must interest adult readers. Standard advice for producing easy reading material had been to manipulate language by the use of short paragraphs, short sentences, active verbs as opposed to passive, and sufficient repetition of words to ensure their fast recognition (Van Horne, pp. 64-65). However, experience had shown that rules such as these cannot be universally applied to all languages. For instance, a publication in the Carib language of Guatemala had been carefully reworked to incorporate as many of the above elements as possible in order to ensure easy reading for new literates in that language. Sentences had been shortened or broken up to form two sentences or more instead of one, active verbs were used, and synonyms were omitted in favor of the use of only one word repeated over and over in the text. According to the rules, it should have been easy to read, but it was not. The Carib people found it extremely difficult to read the choppy, unnatural sentence structure which did not follow their speech style. The constant repetition of the same word was boring. In short, the book was a failure. Their experience matched observations of other SIL colleagues working in other languages, confirming the idea that it is highly important that style of written material conform to a style that is basic to the particular language. Forcing the use of another mode will complicate the reading process rather than facilitate it. (See Chapter 10 for a fuller reference to the development of a written style.)

It was decided at the workshop to discard standard advice and to try a new approach to the definition of graded reading material. Focus was now placed, not upon manipulation of language, but upon relationship of content to the local culture, and upon the specific statement that the author should be a member of the same society as the readers.

Ease or difficulty of reading was determined by the theme's proximity to or distance from the local culture, and according to the way the content is experienced by the author, either personally, or "vicariously," i.e. through research or other secondhand experience.

The easiest reading material has a content which is already well known to both the author and readers. The content theme lies very close to the heart and mind of both author and readers, to the extent that the words may be largely predictable by the new reader (Stage 1).

Activities of the "outside world" which have been personally experienced and which are then presented by the authors to other members of their ethnic group are judged to form materials that are one step more difficult to read than are those dealing exclusively with content already known to author and readers (Stage 2).

The third step in the progression toward still more difficult reading is material with content based upon what the authors have learned from others of the outside world, but which they have not experienced personally (Stage 3).

The most difficult reading of all is material about concepts known to another culture, and translated from another language. The translator is limited as to how many liberties may be taken to make the content interesting and clear to the reader. Change of event presentation order, clarification by additional description, change of "slant" or emotional overtone—all may well be prohibited or at best restricted. Thus the material is highly likely to be extremely difficult for the new readers (Stage 4).

The progression of the stages of difficulty in reading are shown in Figure 1 in terms of the readers' experience, the author's experience, and the degree of restriction placed upon the author's form of presentation.

Easy-to-Difficult Reading Material			
Author: Member of local culture; speaker of local language.			
Readers: Members of local culture; speakers of local language.			
Stage	Content in Relation to:		Form of Presentation
	Experience of Reader	Experience of Author	
1	Known	Direct, Personal	Free
2	Unknown	↓	↓
3	↓	Vicarious	↓
4	↓	↓	Translated

Figure 1.

Further description of the stages of literature may help us to see more clearly their relevance in developing the reading skill.

Stage 1 (content completely familiar to author and readers)
Reading material may include proverbs, legends, songs, and stories that are well known to all the society.
Relying upon a few visual cues, new readers confronted with reading material of Stage 1 type of content intuitively know what the new word is likely to be, what the next one is likely to be, and so on. New literates, although still hesitant and insecure in their recently acquired skill, are now able to gain confidence and security in reading, because the skill is working. They know that what they read is making sense. Therefore, they can read. Furthermore, they are interested in what they are reading because the content of the material matches their own experiences. They are enjoying a good measure of success so they continue, finding the process very enjoyable. Soon they are ready to tackle something a little harder, something not quite so easily predictable.

Within Stage 1 there are gradations of reading material, since the reader cannot know all of the writer's experiences even though they may be quite similar to the reader's own. For example, in a society that engages primarily in fishing for its livelihood, one man's fishing trip may on a particular occasion be very different from another man's fishing trip, if something unusual has occurred. Nevertheless, such a story is still considered to fall in the category of "easiest reading" since the essential elements of the narrative—the setting, the procedure, the means, the characters, even the outcome—are all potentially known by the readers. There is no element to be termed "new" in the sense of belonging to another culture. The surprises in the narration are still within the realm of possibility for the reader.

Stage 2 (new content, personally experienced by the author)

The trip taken by the author to another area—the first ride in an elevator, airplane, bus, car, train, launch—all these form excellent material for a Stage 2 narrative by indigenous individuals who experience these things for the first time, and who write their impressions in a way that the "folks back home" can understand and experience them. The first encounter with a hospital, traffic light, telephone, zoo, supermarket, TV, school, anything that falls into the category of the nonlocal world can be a topic of Stage 2 reading material, described as the author sees fit. A classic example is the description of a telephone given by a teenaged Mixtec (Mexico) girl: "A telephone is like a little toy car, with two wheels. You talk into one wheel, and you listen at the same time to the other wheel. You can talk to someone far away, and you can hear him talk to you. And that's what they mean, my mother, when they say 'talk-by-telephone.'"

Stage 3 (new content, vicariously experienced by the author)

One step further removed from personal experience, the reading material now deals with a noncultural topic which the author has learned from sources other than her/his own experience, by reading, personal interview, or other investigative means. Such reading material may incorporate both Stage 2 and Stage 3 elements. For example, if the telephone description given above should be expanded to give further explanation concerning the operation of a telephone company or the electronic transmission of vocal signals, it is likely that the added information would have been obtained from an instructor or by reading from an encyclopedia or books on the subject of telephones. In the explanation, the author is not limited to any single piece of written information, nor to the order in which bits of information are presented in the source material. The author is at full liberty to convey the message in terminology, figures of speech, and explanations that will bear the most meaning for the hearer or reader. The explanation may be full, or the author may present only those bits of information deemed relevant to the experience and previous knowledge of the readers.

Stage 4 (new content, translated from another language by the author)

An illustration of translated material is hardly needed. However, it should be pointed out that definite principles of translation have been developed involving use of figurative language, known concepts, and meaningful terminology—all with the goal of making the translated material sound as much like the reader's own language experience as possible (see Beekman & Callow, 1974). However, translators are restricted in that they may not expand the material in order to give further explanation or insight, nor is there leeway to change the major order of presentation even if such a change might fit better into the local pattern of logic. Stage 4 material, then, is considered to be the most restricted and, therefore, the most likely to be difficult to read.

Thus, easy-to-difficult reading was redefined as being more closely related to cultural function than to simplified language form. As this new concept began to form during the first days of the 1970 workshop, it became clear that authorship should be the responsibility of the native speaker and not of the educator nor of a member of the dominant culture. Change from a preliterate state to a literate state can best come about when impulse for such change comes from within the organism. This does not mean that educators or field linguists have no further responsibility in the literacy-literature field; it means their role is more that of catalyst—one who provides the "spark" that initiates action in another element. "Catalysts" must know their roles well and be very sensitive to "organisms," knowing when to push, when to wait, when to instruct, when to offer suggestions or help, when to applaud, when to correct and, most of all, when to close their eyes to technical imperfection, knowing that improvement will take place as more expertise is developed.

All these elements were touched upon in the workshop although not all were recognized as important or even possible at that time. As the workshop progressed, it gradually became clear to many of the participating linguists that they had a key not only to a wealth of reading material, but to an ongoing, indigenous literacy which was potentially self-sustaining and self-propagating. While many were elated to be able at last to foresee this possibility, they were chagrined that they had not thought of it previously.

None of the field linguists present was prepared for the change of self-image which took place among the trainees by the end of the workshop. One woman, a monolingual nonliterate whose stories were taped and then transcribed by the linguist, wept as she saw the pages transformed into a booklet which contained *her words*. Enormous possibilities began to open up to her—that she could actually communicate in this way was an overwhelming thought. Later reports indicated that she subsequently grasped very quickly the technique of reading and writing in her language, and later on was employed as a teaching assistant in a local literacy program for women.

Another participant, a third grade dropout from the state school, was unable at first to give more than partial responses to questions put by the linguist in an effort to help him figure out what to write. By the end of five weeks he had become a self-possessed young man whose active mind kept producing more and more material. He took special delight in learning to operate the mimeograph and after only one learning session, insisted upon doing the major work himself in turning out a small newsletter in his language. He calmly instructed his sponsoring linguist as to how she would be allowed to help him in the process.

It is interesting to note that recent articles in the *Journal of Reading*, published by the International Reading Association, indicate that educators in the Western World are becoming increasingly concerned about their students' reading for content. Apparently they sense that an overemphasis has been placed on mastery of the *mechanics* of decoding, with insufficient attention being paid to understanding and action upon the *message* the author wishes to convey.

Jill Sweiger Lewis (1979), in discussing the problem of reading in the content areas, makes specific reference to the necessity of matching reading material with the reader's own background if a satisfying reading experience is to take place.

> The reading act often merely confirms and gives more structure to concepts for which readers already have rich semantic reference ... A reader of limited experiences and thus a narrower framework in the content area customarily experiences frustration and failure . . . . Reading is a disappointing activity because the student is unable to connect the material read with other life experiences. (Lewis, 1979:114).

If the principle of matching book content with a student's background is important in the American educational context, how much more important is the same principle in introducing reading to a preliterate society. And yet the Western World's drive to teach that society how to "live better" is very strong. In fact, it is likely that 95 percent of the readers of this chapter, if actually placed in the position of agent of change in a preliterate society, would begin a literature/literacy program with a booklet designed to improve some area of that society's physical life.

It is hoped that the remaining 5 percent of the readers would 1) begin where the preliterate people are, and 2) help the community to take that first step themselves by writing the first pages ever to be written in that language.

Summary of Desired Goals

Subsequent workshops have affirmed and expanded the insights gained in 1970. We can now state that if a preliterate society is to gain a clear grasp of what is involved in reading and writing, several basic concepts must come into clear focus in the thinking and experience of the target society. These concepts include the realizations that

1. all languages are vehicles of communication, not worthy versus unworthy languages;
2. reading and writing are vital means of communication;

3. writing as a means of communiction can be done in any language, not just the major language of a country;
4. reading and writing are not just for the elite—it is possible for nearly everyone to attain the skill;
5. individuals can become emotionally involved in what they read;
6. one can learn something vital from reading; and
7. the content of reading material is more important than elaborate format.

References

Beekman, John, Callow, John. *Translating the Word of God.* Grand Rapids, Michigan: Zondervan, 1974.

Duff, Martha. How the Branch Minnow story was written. *Notes on Literacy,* 1975, *12*, 21. (Reprinted in *Notes on Literacy, selected articles,* 1979, 225.)

Herzog, Dorothy. A literature workshop, part I, part III. *Notes on Literacy,* 1974, *17*, 1-6; 16-22. (Reprinted in *Notes on literacy, selected articles,* 1979, 226-230; 241-246.)

Lewis, Jill Sweiger. Directed discovery learning: Catalyst to reading in the content areas. *Journal of Reading,* May 1979, *22*, 714-719.

Sealey, Leonard, Sealey, Nancy, Fillmore, Marcia. *Children's writing: An approach for the primary grades.* Newark, Delaware: International Reading Association, 1979.

Van Horne, Marion. *Write the vision.* New York: Committee on World Literacy and Christian Literature, n.d.

Wendell, Margaret M. A literature workshop, part II, *Notes on Literacy,* 1974, *17*, 6-16. (Reprinted in *Notes on literacy, selected articles,* 1979, 231-240.)

Wendell, Margaret, M. An experimental project for production of reading material in a preliterate society. *Notes on Literacy,* 1975, *18*, 1-9. (Reprinted in *Notes on literacy, selected articles,* 1979, 218-224.)

Chapter Three

Elements of a Writer Training Program

There are three principal elements involved in an indigenous writer training program: the trainer, the ethnic community, and the trainee. Attention is focused first upon these human elements rather than upon details of training sessions, which will be discussed later. It should be stressed that the human factors and their interrelationships are of equal or greater importance than the actual training.

Each element is as important as its counterparts and must be considered carefully as to preconceived biases, cultural background leading to present desires and inclinations or disinclinations, and any natural abilities which may be directed toward effecting the desired goals.

The field linguist in the role of trainer will be considered a catalyst rather than a director, and an introducer and resource person rather than a doer.

The community will be seen as the "host" in which the new element (reading and writing) may grow and develop into a self-contained conceptual reality. In order to ensure that the host will be favorable to such growth, it is important that the new element be introduced to the community in a way that is compatible with present cultural norms.

The trainee will be described as the one who has a native speaker's knowledge of and love for the language in which he/she will write, and an equally deep understanding and love for the culture within which she/he writes. Facility and freedom of verbal expression are of equal importance but may not be immediately apparent. Previous schooling, while perhaps helpful, is of secondary importance.

The Trainer

The field linguist, coming in contact with a preliterate group and wishing to see that society become literate, must assume the role of a catalyst and not a doer. According to Webster, a catalyst is the element which introduces or precipitates "an action or reaction between two or more persons or forces" in such a way that the desired action is able to proceed effectively. The forces may be designated here as the world of literacy on one hand and a preliterate people on the other. For action or reaction to take place effectively, grounds of agreement must be discovered and developed until there is a compatible merging of the elements. Obviously, there is a need for someone to discover those common grounds, thus facilitating the desired development.

The following paragraphs briefly describe major areas of which field linguists should be aware in the role of catalyst so that literacy may proceed effectively in a preliterate society.

1. Field linguists first see themselves as listeners, questioners, and learners, but not as instructors. It is absolutely essential that they become acquainted first with the physical community, its members, its leaders, and its system of relationships. More important, an understanding must be gained of its belief system, including its taboos. Otherwise, introduction of reading and writing could inadvertently violate the system and create an atmosphere of fear, distrust, and even hostility which could take years to overcome.

Underlying the study should be the constant question: "How can reading and writing be most meaningfully introduced to this community?" At the same time, the field linguist must be very careful not to answer his/her own question in the way appearing most reasonable on the surface.

This period of investigation and questioning may last much longer than members of our society are willing to endure. While becoming acquainted with the community, field workers with the Cuiba people in Colombia demonstrated their own activity of reading and writing for six years before finding the necessary spark of interest. Because of their patience they saw in the next four years a swiftly-spreading flame of interest in reading and writing which became a fire, revolutionizing the Cuiba community. The long period of restraint paid off handsomely.

2. If the target community must deal in some way with a major or dominant community or society, it is essential that the field linguist become acquainted with the views and objectives of the larger group as well. The catalyst carries the responsibility for knowing characteristics of both elements, if the minor element is eventually to operate comfortably with the major.

3. Indepth acquaintance with the target community implies a good speaking ability in the local language. Otherwise the involvement of the catalyst will be on an extremely superficial level. Trust, respect, and confidence rarely are established firmly without direct communication. Ability to communicate with the dominant society is important as well.

4. Field linguists see themselves as trainers of doers, not as doers. A piece of literature might be produced in short order by the field worker, but its usefulness in the ongoing continuum would end. The community might possibly show interest in the well-turned-out booklet but would its members feel that it was *theirs*, if they had had no involvement in its production?

5. The wise trainer will recognize that a community may go through a five phase period before a new behavior is adopted (Havelock and Havelock, 1973:21). The phases are: awareness, interest, evaluation, trial, and adoption.

Applying these phases to the field of literacy, we can see that a community must first of all be *aware* of the existence of reading material, the content of which must hold great *interest* for the community, and the format of which must be within their eventual reach. Having become aware of and interested in this new element, the community will then *evaluate* it for its relevance to life as the community knows it and lives it. Basing action upon that evaluation, the community will either decide to *try* learning the process of reading and writing and of producing its own materials, or it will abandon the idea, perhaps never to consider it again. If in the trial period, however, the production of written material matches the existing belief and value system, stirs sufficient curiosity and interest, and achieves a good measure of success, the final *adoption* period must follow. The wise trainer realizes that the early phases are crucial for determining final outcome.

6. The successful trainers are planners, able to establish and stick to both long- and short-term goals. They involve the community in establishing these goals, with close observation of community reaction to the short-term goals, adjusting the latter as necessary. They also keep in mind the five phases of adoption and their planning allows time for these to occur, with periodic evaluation as to whether they are occurring and why.

7. Successful trainers are aware of the principle of "synergy" in effecting change, and use it to the advantage of the program. Havelock and Havelock (p. 57) explain synergy as follows:

> Learning seems to take place most forcefully when a number of inputs or stimuli from different sources converge on one point. This is the principle of synergy. The simplest example of synergy occurs when two separate individuals give the same piece of advice. Two inputs from two different sources are far more persuasive than the same input from only one source. In a sense, synergy produces a validation of experience.

The principle of synergy may be seen as an explanation of the current interest now taken in reading among the Mazahaus of Mexico.

After many years of patiently providing several different kinds of literature for the Mazahuas, during which time little interest was shown in reading, the field linguists have now suddenly found themselves selling books by the thousands. What has happened? Why has such avid interest in reading sprung up after many years of apathy?

At about the time of the completion of the largest work, the New Testament, a local radio station discovered it was obligated by federal decree to provide a certain amount of time each week to cultural programs in the local indigenous languages, of which Mazahua is one. The station managers contacted the linguistic team, requesting their assistance. The team in turn contacted certain men of the community who had learned to read and write Mazahua, and assisted them in writing and recording scripts for radio broadcast. As a result, radios in homes all over the Mazahua area were eagerly turned on for the weekly fifteen minute program in Mazahua. The important factor was not so much the content of the program as the realization that the radio station considered the Mazahua language to be worthy of use on the air. Some of the books—such as the dictionary, various locally-authored stories, and a 250 page reading primer—were advertised over the air as being available for purchase. Thus books in Mazahua took on the same value as other items advertised by radio.

Still another force entered the picture. A year or two after the beginning of the radio broadcast in Mazahua, the Federal Department of Education extended its Bilingual-Bicultural Education Program to include certain schools in the Mazahua area. Thus, attention by another source was paid to local language and to reading in the local language. Reading in Mazahua suddenly became the "in" thing, proving the validity of synergistic effect.

8. The trainer seeks to discover the informal opinion leaders of a community, and pays close attention to what they are saying. These opinion leaders may well be the ones to publicize and promote a literacy and literature program. Their early involvement in a program may be crucial to its success.

9. The trainer looks for any sparks of interest manifested in individuals or in the community as a whole, and seeks to relate the interest to reading material as quickly as possible.

10. Trainers know and respect the existing authority structure of both the community and the dominant society. They envision the acceptance of reading and of reading material as occurring within the existing social system, ordered by the existing authority structure. An example of the worth of paying attention to the hierarchical system of authority is found in the Tlapanec situation (Mexico).

After preparing themselves by learning to communicate in the Tlapanec language and by publishing a limited edition of a small story booklet authored by a Tlapanec person, field linguists investigated the Bilingual-Bicultural Education Program of the area in an effort to cooperate with Tlapanec leaders for the stimulation of reading in the Tlapanec community. A system of mutual cooperation was worked out, and the results have been exceptionally rewarding. Local Tlapanec teachers have become fully involved in perfecting the orthography, in writing, in printing and distributing their materials, and in contributing to the funding of these operations.

It is especially important to note how contact was made with the various elements of hierarchical structure in the

Department of Education (see Figure 2). The field linguists were very careful to study the authority structure, and to defer to proper order. As approval of the materials and of the goal of a literate Tlapanec community was expressed at each level, the field linguists were meticulous in following each directive as to whom they should contact on the next level down the hierarchy, and to carry written authorization to the one in charge of that succeeding level. The results were well worth the time and effort expended.

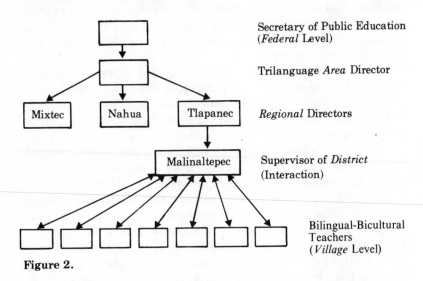

Secretary of Public Education (*Federal* Level)

Trilanguage *Area* Director

Mixtec | Nahua | Tlapanec — *Regional* Directors

Malinaltepec — Supervisor of *District* (Interaction)

Bilingual-Bicultural Teachers (*Village* Level)

Figure 2.

11. The trainer studies the society's problem-solving processes, and follows these processes in resolving difficulties and misunderstandings that are bound to occur. The opinion leaders may be good sources of information as to how these processes operate.

12. The trainer is aware of the many facets of literature production and expects to find individuals within the community who will be able to fill roles required for the total process. For example, a full-blown literacy/literature program may need the following personnel: writers, reporters, editors, publishers, printers, typists, teachers, supervisors, organizers, illustrators, fund-raisers, and catalysts who can introduce the process to other communities. Not all roles will need to be filled

Rationale for Training Indigenous Writers

in initial phases, but their eventual filling must be recognized and planned for. The important factor here is the trainer's anticipation of finding role-fillers within the society.

13. In the periods of evaluation, the wise trainer will remember that evaluation must be made in light of the community's and trainee's background of previous knowledge and experience in reading, writing, and material production. In no case should the trainers consider measuring the materials produced against their own educational or societal background.

It is in the area of evaluation where field workers are most likely to revert to *their* notions of what literature is suitable for production and what is not, and where they may be most severely tempted to impose their value system upon the target society. Western ideas of truth, morality, and printworthiness are far stronger than most of us care to admit. Even so-called liberators have very clear-cut ideas as to the content of reading material.

Judgment is also often imposed on format and quality of production. Unless the process of duplicating materials is taught in a form that can be done on the local scene, the only alternative is to seek a commercial printer.

It is here that the prospect of a self-sustaining indigenous literature begins to slip out of the hands of the local community. It steps into the outside world where it may remain forever buried in the morass of misspelled words (because the language is unfamiliar to the typesetter), illustrations which do not depict the local culture, and a format that costs far more than the local community is able (or willing, at this stage) to support. While access to the commercial printshop may be the solution to forthcoming larger editions, the field worker must recognize that in the early stages of literature production it may be much better to introduce equipment such as the simple "flatbed" silk-screen mimeograph or duplicator (see Appendix C). By learning how to use such relatively uncomplicated equipment, local people will come to understand firsthand how the process works, what details must be considered for printing, and what labor is entailed. At the end of a workshop, the Mundurukú (Brazil) writers resolved to instigate reading classes in their villages so there would be readers to appreciate their booklets and their hard work would not be wasted. They probably never would have thought of pushing reading instruction had the hard work of printing been taken out of their hands. But since they personally had been involved, they saw the need for another highly important phase and proposed taking responsibility for it. What more could a field worker want?

The Community

Centering a literacy/literature program upon a community and its aims and desires is advisable if successful "catalysis" is to take place. An example of centering a program upon a community is found in the Guhu-Samane (Papua New Guinea) education program begun in 1957. A report of the project (Harrison, 1975) indicates that in eighteen years the literacy rate had risen from zero to 62 percent. Furthermore, there is strong evidence that the Guhu-Samane people are fully capable and willingly active in continuing the literature production and the reading program, using their own resources.

Several favorable factors were found in the early stages of the work. Previous contact with the Guhu-Samane people by Lutheran missionaries had been positive, although it had not led to their learning to read. Because the earlier contact had been so positive, a strong demand for reading classes was made as soon as the SIL team arrived. The demand grew, even though the team had not had time to learn the language sufficiently well to enable them to produce teaching materials in it. Nevertheless, the team did what they could, and a few people learned to read. The important factor was that everybody in the community learned to do something in literacy, even if it were only to write one's name or to recognize a few numbers. Thus further positive affirmation was built into the experience of the people. Even when those looking for "cargo" were disppointed at the lack of material wealth forthcoming from the classes, they were satisfied at the field linguists' explanation that the learners had in fact received another kind of cargo. They were assured that what they had learned had been good for the mind, providing food for the inner person, gifts which far surpassed those for the body only.

More satisfactory literacy programs were held later when sufficient time and experience in the language allowed for preparation of better teaching materials. The Guhu-

Samanes grew in their acquaintance with books and what could be learned from them. Fourteen years later the SIL team left the area permanently. The educational program was entirely in the hands of the local leaders, who felt completely competent to handle it without further help from outside.

With respect to formal writer-training, it is important to consult community leaders as to appropriate choice of trainees, topics, and duplication and distribution of materials. The trainees will respond with much better work if they know they have the support of the community, and that they are responsible to the community for good production.

With regard to distribution of literature, it is preferable to involve the community from the very beginning, rather than ask the field linguists to do the selling with the expectation that someone will be inspired to take up the task at a later date. If written material is initially distributed exclusively by the field worker, it is highly likely that, in the minds of the people, literature (or at least the distribution of it) will always be considered to be in the domain of the outsider. Later change-over, or re-identification of distributor will be very difficult.

In certain situations, it may be advisable to involve whatever society is found above the level of the minority language group. The prestige of having the attention and approval of members of the dominant society may be a deciding factor as to whether the literature in the minority language is accepted by the ones for whose benefit it is intended. Sales of books to the Mazatec people of Mexico have been reported as greatly increased after the Mazatecs saw the Spanish speaking storekeeper or the merchant from outside the area buying a two-language dictionary. Thus a stamp of approval by the dominant society was placed upon the books, and the Mazatecs no longer hesitated to purchase them.

Caution should be taken, however, as to the extent to which members of the dominant society, who have not had the special training nor developed the outlook described earlier in this chapter, are involved in the training of authors in the indigenous language. It has been found that at times they tend to edit the indigenous author's work so that it fits the style and thought patterns of the national language. It was recently reported that a highly trained journalist "assisted" indigenous trainees in producing a newsletter which was to have been in two languages. The resulting paper came out entirely in the national language, with none of the articles recognizable by their authors because of the very heavy editing and "improvement."

Involvement of the representative from the dominant society in an indigenous author-training program must be undertaken with as much care and pretraining of the representative as possible. It is not enough to assume that expressions of deep desire to be of assistance, coupled with much experience in the field of writing, will qualify individuals to be trainers. Just as the expatriate field linguists, national trainers must be fully aware of the worth of the indigenous language on its own merits as a language, of its possibilities for use in writing, of the vast differences in culture and interests, and of the value of self-expression on the part of the indigenous trainee.

The Trainee

The question is often asked, "Who should be chosen for training as writers? Should they be persons who already know how to read and write? How much schooling should they have had?"

There are no pat answers to these questions. However, drawing upon experience and observations made by this writer over the course of seven workshops, and upon the reports of colleagues who have directed many more workshops, there are certain principles upon which all observers tend to agree concerning the type of person who is likely to make a good writer.

Running through all the reports of both formal and informal training is the insistence that the best writings come from those trainees who know their own culture thoroughly, who have recently lived within its physical boundaries, and who love and respect their own society. Very often such prerequisites are found in those who have had little or no education in a national school. The process of going through several years of schooling in a rote fashion (usually because of the language problem) tends to structure and to stultify the thinking, and certainly to restrict creative patterns which might emerge as individuals become adept and free in their own language. In effect, they have been studying to become members of another society and are no longer able to relate thoroughly and effectively to their own society.

It is not always true, of course, that the indigene who has had some schooling has little hope of becoming a good writer. The most productive creative writer in Totonac (Mexico) was a young man who had almost completed his secondary school training in Spanish. However, because he had a deep inner commitment to his Totonac culture and was fascinated by his own language, he had always had a deep desire to write in Totonac. To be given the freedom and the help to fulfill his desire was to him a release from the old and an entrance into a brand new world. Apparently the education he had received was no hindrance whatsoever. He had very little trouble escaping from the structure of national language and cultural norms.

The above example is an exception to the rule that education stultifies creativity in the indigenous language. The usual pattern is typified by a report concerning a Cuicatec (Mexico) writer who could "just reach out and 'grab' the most appropriate word." This man was monolingual and noneducated in the local school system.

While education may or may not be a hindrance in the development of an indigenous author, the primary factor should be on trainees' potential for command of their own language, and on their total involvement in the culture about which and to which they are writing.

There are born storytellers in every society, as well as artists, managers, leaders, followers, and teachers. Whatever generalized role is found in Western society, its counterpart will be found in a preliterate society. Probably it is easier to locate the raconteur than many of the other roles, since storytelling often fills a prominent part in a preliterate society. This may be the place to start—with individuals known for their entertaining tales. Problems may arise, especially with the elderly who do not wish to become involved in committing their work to paper. In that case, it may be feasible for a younger person to help with the actual recording and/or transcription of the material given by an elder. The field linguist working among the Wolaamo (Ethiopia) found that teaching young men, who had been away from the group for several years while attending school, to transcribe stories told by older people helped these young men to get back into the thought patterns of the society and to recall the forms of expression which were peculiar to the society as well as deeply meaningful.

The elders of the Amuesha group (Peru) have decided among themselves that leadership in any activity where reading, writing, or general schooling is concerned should be in the hands of the younger men. Older people lend their approval and support and act as resource people, but leave the actual decision-making to the young leaders.

As in any other culture, thoughtful, creative persons—those who have a way with words and who delight in being articulate, the innovative, and the fearless who, though deeply appreciative of their culture are still willing to attempt something new—make the most promising trainees.

Should the trainee always be a man? Might a woman be chosen? The answer to this depends to a large extent upon the society and the place it gives to women. If the first reading material to be seen is that written by a woman, and the society is heavily male-oriented, then a literacy/literature movement is likely to come to an abrupt halt. However, the choice of women trainees in certain groups in Guatemala has worked out quite well. In one case a woman writer has become an instructor in subsequent courses; she is well received and respected in the role.

Several reporting teams have mentioned that it is much more satisfactory to train more than one writer at a time. A team of four to six is about ideal. Many indigenous people have become accustomed to working in teams, and they perform much more comfortably and happily than when working alone.

What about teenagers? Do they make good writers? While there are always exceptions to the rule, reports indicate that youthful writing is not usually the best for an initial literature. Consensus indicates that they simply have not experienced life long enough to be able to produce the literature needed in an introductory stage in a society. However, it is important that they not be discouraged from attempting to write but, rather, that ways be found to make use of their skills and eagerness to participate. They could be the prolific writers of tomorrow if given positive experiences today.

Above all other factors influencing the choice of writer-candidates, the most important is that community leaders have a part in making that choice. The trainees thus know that they have community support and also have a responsibility to produce, for the community is going to be interested in the materials they write.

It has been found that local leaders are far more capable than nonlocal field linguists choosing the right people to be trained as *teachers*, since they are far more familiar with individual innate qualities and of social positions which must not be ignored. It may be more difficult, however, for the leaders to pick out potential *writers*, for qualifications may be harder to define. Therefore, it may be that the leadership itself should first be given some kind of in-depth introduction to the process. Care must be taken, of course, that in no way do they experience "loss of face." For leaders to fail in any way would be disastrous not only to them but to an ongoing program.

The town president in one particular community was clearly not in favor of any kind of a literacy/literature program since he was convinced that the language of the town could not be written. The field linguists made a special point of producing some reading material as early as possible, i.e., within the first three months of the study of the language. The titles were *How We Make a Cornfield* and *Butchering a Pig*. (The latter is still in demand for purchase by the people.) Of course they made a gift of the booklets to the president before any of the people saw them. When the president held the material in his own hands, and found that his previous schooling in Spanish allowed him to read it with only a little additional instruction, his negative attitude became positive almost immediately. He even volunteered to write several stories which were later used in a primer to introduce vernacular reading to those who could already read Spanish. By participation, he demonstrated his approval and in so doing set a tone of cooperation for the community. The team then was able to progress more rapidly in all projects.

Summary

The most important part of a training program is not the program itself but the human element involved, and the relationships that develop among the trainer, the community, and the trainees.

Trainers must see their own roles in proper perspective: they are catalysts, not doers. They must be constantly aware that attention should focus not on *their* work but on the accomplishments of the community and its members.

The active cooperation of the community must be sought early in choosing trainees for writing and for the many other roles which a local literature production program will demand. Unless community leaders can sense that they control the lines of authority, the prospect is dim for an indigenous literature program's development.

Finding people who will make good writers is not easy, for the role is a new one in a preliterate society. Of primary importance, the trainees must be those who know and love their own culture and who are not ashamed of it. This takes precedence over a background of formal education. Local leaders may be able to pinpoint the likeliest candidates, providing they themselves understand what is involved.

References

Harrison, J. Daniel. Community education among the Guhu-Samanes. *Papua New Guinea Journal of Education*, 1975, *2*, 26-30. (Reprinted in *Notes on Literacy*, 1978, *23*, 1-5.)

Havelock, Ronald G., and Havelock, Mary C. *Training for change agents.* Ann Arbor, Michigan: The University of Michigan Institute for Social Research, 1973.

Chapter Four

Informal and Formal Training

Examples of Informal Training

The most desirable context for training native authors is their own locale, where they live and move freely. The advantage of informal, on-the-spot training is that it can take place at almost any time, in almost any place, thus creating an immediate and meaningful relationship beween reading or writing and life's experience. Details are fresh in the speaker's mind and much less effort is needed to put the experience into writing than if he must wait for a formal training or writing period.

The aforementioned incident concerning the Amuesha (Peru) story of the minnow which was rescued after being flipped out of a bucket of water illustrates how a seemingly insignificant experience can be turned into a literary contribution to a program which perhaps has not yet begun. Nevertheless, its effect can be far-reaching. Today, children studying in the Amuesha bilingual school have become so well aware of turning "happenings" into written form that they regularly carry notebooks with them so they can quickly write down incidents or thoughts which cross their way or their minds. As a result, the Amuesha library shelf is gradually being filled with booklets. Its very existence confirms the value of such informal training done at an early stage. The Amuesha are literate and know the joy of being so. They are fully capable of independently propagating this element in their lives for many years to come. It takes little imagination to foresee the value of full-fledged literacy as the Amuesha adjust to changing lifestyles.

The Piros, another group living in the Peruvian jungle, were encouraged to write whatever they desired even while they were learning the skills of reading and writing. Like the Amuesha, they were introduced to the idea of written communication on a very informal level. Subsequent formal education (bilingual schools) supplemented and reinforced the skill, but the idea of personal involvement in the production of written material had already been well established in community thinking.

Reading and writing began among the Cuiba people of Colombia with a teenaged boy, who for six years had watched field linguists who seemed to be forever occupied with things called paper and pencils. One day the youth requested a pencil, which was given to him. The next request was, "How do I use it?" Thus began the first writing lesson which turned naturally into a reading lesson. Within twenty hours of instruction the boy mastered the process. It was not long before the idea spread to others, and a program was born. This does not mean that it immediately grew without further nurturing. The team fed it constantly and one of their projects did, indeed, require much time and effort on their part. When they left the Cuiba area for a few months to attend intensive linguistic courses at a study center, they spent much of their spare time writing letters to all the people of the community. No postal system was operative in that part of the jungle at the time, so the field linguists had to find those who might be traveling through the vicinity, and who would be able to deliver the letters for them. It was not a simple process, but it paid off. These letters excited a great deal of interest among the people, and also provided a model for them to follow. As people progressed toward literacy they began writing notes to the field linguists, and then to each other. It is reported that often a man who was working at some distance from his house would send a note home to his wife, even though he might return home in a few hours. In some cases, the wife had not yet learned to read but she knew that a message was being conveyed, and she hurried to find someone who could read it to her. Thus it became well established in community thinking that reading was communication, that it was exciting and meaningful, and that they themselves could participate in it. It was no longer just a meaningless activity that one observed among strangers.

Because the Cuibas had been so well trained on the informal level they caught on very quickly to typing, mimeographing, and booklet or newsletter production when they attended a multilingual workshop later. Here they were able even to assist those of other groups in the acquisition of many of the technical skills.

Such progress may not seem remarkable until one reflects that, only a few years before, the Cuibas had been completely nomadic people whose only possessions were things such as canoes and hammocks which they had made. They had no cooking pots or clothing. Life was sustained entirely by food obtained in hunting and fishing. Only thirteen years after initial contact with the linguists, the Cuibas are currently in the process of establishing a stable community. They are writing their own materials and conducting their own school. The Cuiba example clearly demonstrates the effectiveness of capturing the moment when interest is exhibited and of turning such interest into activity relevant to the ultimate goal—a literate society. Informal teaching, done at the very instant when one spark of interest was shown, was the key to a total literacy program which shows every indication of becoming highly successful in a minimal length of time.

Another example of using a spur-of-the-moment incident as an occasion for stimulating creative writing concerns the Usarufa people of Papua New Guinea.

The first creative writing occurred when we returned to the village after an absence of several months. Everyone was eager to tell us something we had missed out on. Seizing the opportunity, we said, "Don't tell us. Go home and write it." That was the birth of the first short stories in Usarufa. Some were excellent. (Vida Chenoweth)

The changes brought about in the community of the Sepik-Iwam, also of Papua New Guinea, illustrate the value of local training with community involvement. Here the federal government had attempted several times to start a school in Pidgin English, always with the same result: the departure of the teachers in discouragement and defeat. A very rigorous climate (hot, humid jungle river area) to which they were not accustomed, plus utter disinterest by the people in what they had to teach, were sufficient to discourage even the most dedicated teachers. It was a multitude of letters, written in Sepik-Iwam and scattered over the village from the window of a small airplane, that finally aroused interest in reading. The letters had been sent by the field linguist who was at the central base of operations, but who had not forgotten the need of the Sepik-Iwam to learn to read. Frustrated because they could not read the messages the letters contained, the people asked the linguist when she returned to the area to tell them what she had wanted them to know. Instead of merely reading the letters, she feigned great surprise that the recipients could not read them for themselves. "I wrote the letters in your language—why didn't you read them?" At this point it began to dawn upon the people that the "carvings" really did represent their language, that they could be decoded and understood, and that the message could be vitally interesting.

Enthusiasm in reading and writing classes began to mount. At the same time the start of a spiritual awakening helped the people to have open minds toward new ideas. Now, some ten years later, a large building has been erected by the community itself with some outside financial assistance. It houses a school taught by Sepik-Iwam teachers, with classes for children and adults. In addition, there are smaller classrooms where intensive writer-training courses are held periodically to stimulate the flow of materials. Five cubicles are reserved for Sepik-Iwam men who are translating the New Testament and who need a place where they will be undisturbed. It is highly unlikely that the group will ever fall back into illiteracy, for they themselves control the program, and they make it highly relevant to their lives.

Showing a potential writer what has been done by other groups is a key method for obtaining material, reports the team studying the Southern Tepehuan language of Mexico:

> Tom showed the language teacher books done in other indigenous languages, which inspired him to "tell it like it is" in his area. He became so familiar with the idea of writing that when a funny incident happened at home, he immediately told Tom about it the next morning so they could record and transcribe it. (Thomas and Elizabeth Willett)

Booklets composed of several such stories proved to be very popular among the Southern Tepehuan people. "They are as much interested in indigenous literature as in the colorful *National Geographic*. Most of the first five books we published sold out within the first year." It should also be pointed out that the booklets were sold at cost, not at subsidized prices, even though the economic state of the Southern Tepehuan people is no higher than that of other rural areas of Mexico.

The natural creativity of the Tepehuan language teacher and writer was a vital factor in the production of highly interesting material. However, the talent was not apparent to the field linguists when they began learning the language and teaching the instructor to read and write. The important element was that the linguists *expected* to discover talent, and they did. "This particular teacher is especially talented and creative anyway. He just needed coaching to bring him out." The linguist who does not expect to find latent talents in the community will probably have little success uncovering them.*

The endorsement and participation of an "authority figure" among the Wapishanas of Guyana was the key to abundant literature production. The team had first published a book of Wapishana legends which had been recorded on tape and transcribed. These did not provide sufficient motivation to inspire further writing, or even an interest in learning to write at this early stage. At a later date, however, interest was aroused when a course of study was presented to adults who had previously learned to read and write in English. A major key to success here was that the course was backed by the head teacher of the school and by the village chief and had been organized by the chief's grandson, who was himself a leading and enthusiastic participant.

After the first writing assignment, we never had to give one. Once they found they could do it, we were kept busy

---

*Georgia Hunter, my colleague in Mexico, has remarked that there are two kinds of sponsoring field linguists who bring trainees to writer workshops. One expects that the trainees will produce good material, and the other expects that the effort will be too much for them. Expectations are fulfilled for both types.

going over the stories they brought each day . . . . We ended up with a sixty-four page book, consisting of Wapishana stories in the front, their English translation in the back. This is our most popular book even though it is the most expensive. (Beverly Dawson)

A truly ongoing system of literature production is still an objective to be reached among the Wapishana, but good groundwork has been laid.

Learning to type sparked creative writing among the Guarani of Brazil. The Guarani people had observed reading and writing for several years, and some had learned something of the skills in Brazilian schools conducted in Portuguese. Nothing had promoted writing in the mother tongue nor in Portuguese. As in so many other societies where a minority language is spoken, reading and writing simply had no involvement in their lives.

The following incident initiated a change:

A very shy 15-year old boy sat in our living room almost every day for three weeks without saying much of anything. Finally Bob remembered having told him that he would bring back a typewriter (from a recent trip outside), and wondered if he was wanting to learn to type. That was exactly what he wanted, but he was too shy to ask. After the first week of typing lessons, the day before he finished learning all the keys, he brought a short story he had written in his own language. We encouraged him and others to write and soon they brought a number of stories. This typing experience not only opened the door to locally authored materials, but made everyone want to read and write so they could learn to type. (Robert and Kathie Dooley)

The first books in Narak of Papua New Guinea were made from transcribed texts previously recorded by Narak speakers. Although they had not yet learned to read and write, they identified the books as "theirs" because they had furnished the illustrations as well as the stories.

The Kasem people of Ghana were stimulated to write stories simply by being asked. Folk stories were sought first, then childhood experiences were requested as material for a teacher-training course. "The material flowed out! . . . We plan to start producing a mimeographed newsletter so we can make use of these stories before requesting more."

Very brief, one-line notes by the field linguists were the introductions to writing among the Nambiquara people of Brazil. To supplement regular writing exercises in the literacy classes, new readers received written messages such as "We are going to bathe now." "I'm going to cook now." or "My child wants to play ball with you." These notes eventually stimulated notes back to the field linguists—"I'm going hunting now. I will be back for school tonight." This grew to become an exchange of letters among the Nambiquara people, even to regular written interchanges between villages. So very serious an element has this become in the life of the Nambiquara, that the chief has exhorted them to "write only true words—never lies."

Among the Choco of Panama, the field linguist made creative writing a part of a beginning literacy class:

> After we had gone through the first primer . . . I asked the students to write down three sentences of their own making to bring to class each day. Later they formed these sentences into little stories, and finally illustrated the stories. At each of these steps they had great misgivings. They were sure that they could never think of a sentence to write, could never make a story, and of course they thought they could never draw anything either. I just told them that this all belonged to learning, that they could at least try. So they tried, and got praise for every effort. We made all the stories into a booklet. How proud they were when they held the mimeographed copy of their very own writing in their hands. (And my coworker and I were no less thrilled!) . . . We showed the book to any Choco-speaking passerby, hoping it would encourage others to learn to read and write too. One man got so excited that he went home and wrote a whole booklet of stories himself. Another immediately followed his example and wrote two booklets. (Edil Rasmussen)

Most of the foregoing examples come from geographically isolated, nonsophisticated groups. In contrast, the Agni of Ivory Coast represent a very different situation. Far from being isolated and monolingual, the Agni can boast of several professional writers of international status writing in French.

Great interest in writing in Agni was shown by speakers of that language as soon as the field linguists began to study it, so they quickly set about turning that interest into action. After making a preliminary orthography, they prepared a twelve-page booklet as a writer's orthographical guide, in order to test the new alphabet. The booklet contained a list of all the letters and letter combinations with several key words as examples with the French gloss for each. A brief grammatical section contained one complete verb conjugation, examples of punctuation, and other orthographical conventions. A traditional folktale, some proverbs, and an original short story (written by one of the language teachers) were included as samples of literature desired. Several small groups put the booklet to use, and produced a number of stories. Through these small, informal writing groups, the field linguists were able to determine that there were several young men who had special talent for writing. They later arranged for seven of the Agni speaking men to attend a primer-making workshop combined with a writing seminar.

> Three young men wrote a first draft primer and teacher's guide and a sixty-three page primer for semiliterates and for those already literate in French. The others produced the first three published books in Agni....The primer for semiliterates was attractively illustrated by one of the workshop participants. (Jonathan and Nancy Burmeister)

Thus, both local training and a more formalized training were used to produce the desired results of trained writers and literature production.

Evidence of spontaneous writing among the Wik-Munkan group of Australia has been meager. However, the hymns and the few letters that have been written deserve more notice than perhaps would be merited if they came from a group in another country. Like other Australian Aborigine groups, the Wik-Munkan have been taught to disparage their own language to an alarming degree. That they are interested in writing anything at all in their language is most encouraging and shows hope that they will one day be able to identify themselves as proud speakers of their language.

Formalized Training: Workshops

Despite the acknowledged desirability of training indigenous authors by informal methods applied as opportunity arises, many colleagues of the Summer Institute of Linguistics have found such training difficult to carry out. The second most efficient method has been to conduct training by means of formal workshops in which a group of trainees learns the fundamentals of writing and printing. They learn how to carry the procedure through from initial writing to completion in duplicated form.

The workshops are considered formal training in that there is a regular schedule to be followed, classes that the trainee must attend, deadlines to be met, and objectives to be attained.

In some cases, workshop training has been found to be advantageous in comparison with the informal type given in the trainee's locale. The act of following a formal procedure often conveys deep satisfaction to the member of a preliterate society who may have had little or no opportunity to attend school. Furthermore, the certificate awarded in a closing ceremony may be the first that person has ever received. Contact and fellowship with other trainees of different backgrounds may be stimulating intellectually to a writer-in-training who perhaps has had little such contact previously.

At this writing, it is impossible to state definitely the number of writer-training workshops which have been conducted under the auspices of the Summer Institute of Linguistics. It is estimated that there were 35-50 such workshops conducted between 1970 and 1978.

Concerning content of workshop training, I have drawn upon conversations or correspondence with directors or coordinators of workshops, as well as upon more formal reporting of SIL workshop activity in Australia, Bolivia, Brazil, Colombia, Ghana, Guatemala, Ivory Coast, Mexico, Nepal, Nigeria, Panama, Peru, the Philippines, and the United States.

It is again impossible to define the ideal length of time that a writer-training workshop should run. Those reported have ranged in length from three days to three months, depending upon the degree of readiness of the trainees to profit from the teaching, and upon the time available to spend on such a project. However, most workshop leaders indicate preference for a period of five to six weeks for training beginning writers in all steps of the process.

Usually the workshops are held in a semirural setting, often at a center operated by the Summer Institute of Linguistics especially for concentrated language study. Such centers provide adequate housing and study facilities for both sponsoring linguists and writer-trainees. These study centers are usually located a short distance from urban areas in order to avoid the disturbances of city life. At the same time, it is helpful to be close enough to sources of supply that the procurement of food and other commodities is not a problem.

Workshop activity focuses upon the trainees, with eight types of activity usually scheduled: 1) discussion sessions, 2) typing classes, 3) use of the duplicator, 4) writing time, 5) consultations with instructors, 6) art classes, 7) excursions, 8) social events.

More advanced workshops have included the teaching of some practical activity such as making compost for vegetable gardens, grafting fruit trees, raising rabbits for meat, constructing portable ovens, and making bread. These projects also provide subjects for writing.

Seminars are usually offered also to the field linguists who sponsor and assist the trainees at the workshop, depending upon the amount of previous exposure they have had to the objectives and procedures of training indigenous authors.

Writer-training workshops often have provided enough stimulation and sufficient expertise that field linguists or trainees or both are able to instigate further training courses in the home village. By the end of a workshop, field linguists and trainees must be convinced that ongoing production of literature is essential if the society is to become truly literate, and that achievement is possible by the society in question. To promote such attitudes, the director and teaching personnel of such a workshop must be encouraging, supportive, and especially innovative in seeking ways of developing the desired attitudes.

For a detailed description of activities directed to both trainees and field linguists, the reader is referred to Part Two of this book.

Summary

Both informal and formal training of indigenous writers have proven effective. The insight and ingenuity of the field linguists are more prominent in informal training, in that they must be ready to seize casual opportunities to focus attention on reading and writing.

The more formal (i.e., in a workshop) training also offers advantages such as prestige, influence, and example. These may convey greater significance to the trainee than that which is offered locally on a casual basis. Most significantly, trainees often gain sufficient competence and confidence that they, in turn, can provide training for others.

SOURCES

Language	*Field Linguists**
Agni (Ivory Coast)	Jonathan and Nancy Burmeister
Amuesha (Peru)	Martha Duff Tripp, Mary Ruth Wise
Choco (Panama)	Edil Rasmussen (Baptist Mission)
Cuiba (Colombia)	Isabel Kerr, Marie Berg
Guarani (Brazil)	Robert and Kathie Dooley
Kasem (Ghana)	Philip and Judy Hewer
Nambiquara (Brazil)	Menno and Barbara Kroeker
Narak (Papua New Guinea)	Joan Hainsworth, Kay Johnson
Piro (Peru)	Esther Matteson, Joyce Nies
Sepik-Iwam (Papua New Guinea)	Marilyn Laszlo
Southern Tepehuan (Mexico)	Thomas and Elizabeth Willett
Usarufa (Papua New Guinea)	Vida Chenoweth
Wapishana (Guyana)	Beverly Dawson
Wik-Munkan (Australia)	Ann Curnow Eckert, Christine Kilham

*Members of the Summer Institute of Linguistics, unless otherwise stated.

Chapter Five

Results from Four Perspectives

What have been the results of training indigenous writers? Is there any merit in the idea or is it too idealistic to suppose that a preliterate society can, in fact, generate enough interest in self-expression through writing that it can propel itself into the world of written communication?

It is not possible to make a flat statement at this point that training indigenous writers is either a complete success or an utter failure, for it was only ten years ago that the first tentative organizational beginnings were made in the SIL context. And that was in only one country with only a handful of trainees. Even those first steps were not taken with anything like confidence and clarity.

However, as stated in the Introduction, recent reports from SIL workers in 14 countries point more toward success than failure. Respondents to the 1977 letter were by far more positive than they were negative toward the value of training writers. In 1979, it appeared that the idea was still gaining momentum; for example, in one area where the indigenous people have been especially wary of any kind of innovation, it is noteworthy that two of its citizens recently sought an opportunity to attend a writers' workshop, and another requested help in recording on tape some of the area folklore, presumably for transcription into writing.

On my desk before me is a letter from Frances Jackson, an SIL colleague who has conducted several writer workshops for indigenous groups in Colombia.

Upon my return after a year's absence I began getting many reports of independent production of booklets—writing, typing, and mimeographing all being done during the absence of the field linguists. Several groups have started newssheets, and the Guahibo now produce a bimonthly newspaper of 12 pages, the only one in the State and the only minority newspaper registered in Colombia.

Such reports are encouraging, indeed, but commonsense tells us that we must beware of too much optimism. Many a match has flared upon striking, but has failed to light the desired fire. Can these sparks of interest, resulting in display of initiative and ingenuity really carry a preliterate society forward into self-perpetuating literateness? These are auspicious beginnings, but will writing thrive? What will it take to nurture writers until they can operate permanently and independently? Can their influence create a momentum sufficient to carry a major portion of the preliterate society into literateness?

So that every possible encouragement may be given to the writers and to those societies where their own production of material is just beginning to take hold, it will be helpful to look at the results reported thus far. These results will be considered from the points of view of the trainee, the indigenous community, the national educator, and the field linguist.

From the Perspective of the Trainee

New Enthusiasm

Nearly all respondents indicated that they have noted an exuberance of spirit heretofore unseen in the indigenous person. Confidence replaces timidity in some trainees, particularly among those coming from cultures which have long been under the domination of another culture.

In Latin America this new assurance seems to be related primarily to language as realization comes through that the indigenous language can be written and that trainees can write it and through this means express themselves. One budding author in all of his first booklets wrote an introduction expressing his newfound appreciation for his language. Each one included some version of the following:

> . . . there will be no greater satisfaction for the author than to know that the reader has found this booklet interesting, and also that he has discovered that there

is no reason to be ashamed that he speaks an indigenous language. This book is dedicated with much pride to the Totonac race which lives in the Totonicapan area ("Xamanixna" 1974:2, translated).

Following the Introduction is a brief chapter entitled "The Totonac Language." Here the author depicts the sociolinguistic problems faced by Totonac speakers, and urges his readers to become aware of the fact that these beliefs and attitudes have no basis in actuality. He strips away the notion that reading belongs only in the realm of the Spanish language and states that when Totonac people learn to read in Spanish "they only learn to memorize and repeat as a parrot does. But if questions are asked as to what they have learned ... how many questions go unanswered?" (p.6).

He urges initial learning in the Totonac language because "it is our full right to do so in the mother tongue." As to the adequacy of Totonac, he states that it ranks with English, Russian, and other indigenous languages bordering the Totonac area, in that whatever is said in Totonac can be expressed in other languages as well.

As to the value of his language, the only thing wrong with it is that "it has not been given the importance that it should have . . . despite the fact that [it] was spoken for centuries before the Spanish people arrived" (p. 7).

Not all writer-trainees have expressed so volubly their inner frustrations as well as newfound freedom in the context of their own language. Nevertheless, this same feeling has been noted in many of the responses to the 1977 letter.

New Height of Achievement Reached

Along with the newly discovered confidence in language, there is a sense of having achieved the impossible. A most vivid impression was made upon this writer when one of the trainees came to the workshop director's office before leaving for his home village. Thinking of the possible disillusionment he might experience upon returning home, I sought to warn him gently that his booklet might not receive the acclaim that I was sure he was expecting from his fellow villagers. After all, they were not accustomed to reading and might not appreciate its full import. But this usually stolid and matter-of-fact young man would have none of it. With great excitement ringing in his voice and shining through his eyes, he replied, "Oh, they'll like it! They'll like it! You see, there's never ever been anything written in our language—*and I have made the first book!"* He had joined the world of Marco Polo, Thomas Edison, and Neil Armstrong; the thrill of discovery and achievement in the "unknown world" permeated his whole being.

The editor of the aforementioned Guahibo newspaper of Colombia received national acclaim when he was invited to attend an invitation-only party for selected Colombian newspaper journalists on the Day of the Newspaperman. He is also being considered for honorary membership in the most prestigious Colombian newspapermen's association. Out of respect for the pioneering courage and ingenuity of this indigenous writer-editor, it is being suggested that the requirement of a college degree and five years of experience be waived, and an invitation to honorary membership be extended to this man who has had no formal schooling. Visits by journalists and government officials from Bogotá to the rural newspaper office brought forth reports of commendation and praise, not just for the effort expended, but for the intrinsic worth of the newspaper itself.

Personal Advancement

Learning to control reading and writing to new depths has proven economically profitable to some writer-trainees, although the monetary increase has not yet come directly from their writings. (*Never* is such an objective held out to the trainees in the workshops, for it could well prove false.) Nevertheless, many trainees have been found to be ideal candidates for teacher-training and for supervisory positions, particularly in areas where a bilingual-bicultural education system has been adopted. (For further explanation of the system developed in Peru, see Larson, Davis, and Davila, 1979.) Other official positions of leadership, such as town secretary, have been granted to those who have had writer training since they obviously command the skills demanded by such roles.

Initiation of Schools

Some writers have been catalysts for instigation of reading classes. The Munduruku (Brazil) trainees were overheard making plans for teaching reading classes in their villages ". . . so people can read the materials we've worked so hard to produce!"

Development through Experience

Meager experience in the world of books is greatly expanded by the training in writing. Notions of how books come into being are no longer vague and shadowy. One African trainee stated: "I used to think that all you had to do was push a lot of paper into one side of the engine [printing press] and out would come a book from the other side, all written and with its covers pressed down. Now—I *know* how a book is made."

Latent Talents Revealed and Developed

Previously undiscovered natural talents often surface in the process of training writers. In Mexico it was suddenly discovered that a man whom the field linguists had known and worked with for years had exceptional ability in drawing cartoon-like figures. These were both amusing and instructive. What was most remarkable about the discovery was that the man was not a writer trainee, but a visitor to the workshop. He had become inspired to do the series of pictures (casually doodled on the back of an old envelope) upon learning the purpose of the workshop, and the ultimate goal that their indigenous society, as well as others, become self-sustainingly literate. The prospect of such, and the realization that the outsiders—the field linguists—expected and desired this to happen filled him with a new enthusiasm which he expressed in his cartoons.

To cite again the Guahibo newspaper, a recent report tells of the discovery of a "headlines writer." Because demands of the planting season had cut down on newspaper staff, the editor of *La Voz de Cavasí* brought in a new recruit to help with a current issue. To the editor's delight, the recruit was found to have a knack for stating the topic within the space limitation of the column's width—no easy task since Guahibo words are unusually long.

Keesing and Keesing (1971:364) pose the question: "Must members of a minority group reject what is distinctive of their way of life to achieve equal opportunity?" Too often, agencies of change have viewed this rejection of the old as necessary to any kind of progress and have insisted on it. To ward off this result, some societies have closed their doors to all outside influence and activity. One respondent described a certain society that fits well into this category. Much cultural pressure has been exerted to enforce conformity. No one must be allowed to differ from the norm.

Conflict arises between the society and an individual who possesses much innate creativity as well as curiosity. How can this creativity be expressed and curiosity satisfied without violating the society's "rules"? In at least one case, it was recognized that writing within the framework of the local language and culture satisfied both the creative writer and the society which he had no wish to leave nor to violate. Because the content of his writing conformed beautifully to the cultural values, his work was highly acceptable to the community, even praised. At the same time it gave him the expressive outlet that he craved as an individual.

Several respondents indicated that creativity had been "discovered," not "stimulated" nor "developed." The usual method of discovery was simply to offer individuals opportunities to express themselves either verbally or pictorially. Opportunity, with few or no restrictions as to the form of the expression, was all that was needed. Thus, literacy was born.

Poetry is often considered a form that reaches the height of verbal creativity. Unless oral poetry is common in a particular language and culture, can we expect to find it coming from the pen (or typewriter) of an indigenous writer? I believe the answer is yes, we can expect it, but we cannot assign the writing of it as we would a folktale, a personal experience, or some other type of prose writing.

From time to time, beautiful poetry has emerged either during the course of a workshop or later. Such spontaneity of expression can be explained only in that the way was opened for it to come forth from the depths of an individual heart and experience. Such was the case of an Engenni (Nigeria) trainee who had completed a week's course held in his village. A few weeks later he appeared at the linguist's door with a notebook in hand. Here he had recorded his heart's musings, written in prose form. But when it was read aloud the linguist knew that it was poetry. The subject matter dealt primarily with the author's love and respect for the land which gave him his food, awe for the great river flowing by his village, and his deep sorrow for the war which had brought heartache and misery throughout the country. The workshop had opened for this man an avenue for deeply meaningful creative expression in the language of his innermost being. (See Appendix A, Sample 6.)

Thus we see that the writers, themselves, are the first to benefit by their training as authors. Increase in self-esteem, pride in being speakers of a real and ancient language, pleasure in pioneering writing in that language, a new realization that they too can enter the modern world of books, opportunity to express and develop innate creativity—all combine to make such training a coveted experience.

It is no wonder that an individual from a culture that has deliberately warded off all suggestion of change, is now asking for a chance to attend a writer's workshop.

From the Perspective of the Indigenous Community

As locally produced literature slowly begins to be generated, we note that communities as wholes are beginning to respond affirmatively to its import. In this section we will examine some of the advantages oberved from the viewpoint of the indigenous community.

Ethnic Identification

Locally authored literature has been found to be a means of preserving identification with the local culture even while its citizens are gravitating toward another, usually the dominant culture. Contrary to fears expressed by some educators, this sense of linguistic and ethnic identification does not necessarily produce conflict with another culture nor does it make adaptation more difficult. Rather, it enables its citizens to understand themselves and their ways in contrast to the new ways, to choose from the new what will be most beneficial, and to retain from the old that which makes them proud of their identity. This is well illustrated in an SIL report given to the Minister of Education in Suriname, concerning progress of the Arawak people.

> The Arawaks want to see themselves and their children more integrated into the larger Suriname society, but at the same time they continue to value their own culture. They send their children to "town" to obtain a good education but deplore the fact that they sometimes

forget their mother tongue and reject old cultural values. Working with their language, and learning [details of] their own culture were greeted with enthusiasm. They looked at [their language in writing] both as a way of providing a bridge between Arawak and town culture, and as a means of preserving some sort of self-identity for themselves and their descendants.

Similar reports have come from other countries. From Mexico:

[One older man] has been very cooperative in recording folktales because he feels that the older people are no longer adequately passing these on to the younger generation and he thinks having them in books would help that problem.

From Papua New Guinea:

[One of the two most popular books] was on Kanite cultural items . . . . The adults are very pleased with this book because it tells the children about their [customs] which are fast disappearing.

One cannot help but wish that educational authorities, curriculum devisers, and agencies of change would pay more respectful attention to this basic need of a minority group, a need to preserve its linguistic and ethnic heritage, even though that group understands that some incorporation into the national culture is desirable for their own ultimate benefit.

The younger generation, caught in changing cultural patterns, often welcomes a glimpse into the customs of their parents and grandparents, thus gaining insight into one source of familial misunderstanding and conflict. A young Nigerian school teacher, training as a writer in his language, chose to make a booklet concerning changes in customs dealing with marriage, the role of women, and the rearing of children. He compared the old and the new ways under the headings of "Things we used to do long ago" and "Things we copy from others." It was his hope that booklets on such topics would help to restore family relationships which had been damaged because of lack of mutual understanding in the midst of changing lifestyles. Both generations value such booklets since both are accorded the respect, as shown by sympathetic explanation. Although the writer indentified himself as being of the new generation, it is possible that he felt himself actually to be in a kind of cultural no-man's-land. Perhaps his choice of topic revealed his own need to understand his roots.

Vulnerability Reduced

It is obvious that merely being literate does not place a protective coat of armor around a people ensuring that they will never be swindled. However, vulnerability to exploitation is greatly reduced among those for whom reading and writing have become meaningful. An illustration of this principle, operating on a very basic level, comes from South America. One indigenous group—nomadic, monolingual, and completely preliterate—was gradually being pushed further away from their territory. They were losing ancient, though unwritten, claim to the banks of a certain river where they hunted and fished to supply daily food. A burgeoning national population produced colonists who needed land and who coveted the rich, watered river land. Little by little they were claiming jungle areas which appeared to be unclaimed since there were no farms, no villages, nothing visible to indicate that they belonged to anyone.

In the past few years, however, the largest band of the indigenous group had become fascinated with the reading and writing of their own language, and because of this new development, a different lifestyle began to form. They decided to settle down in one section along the river so they could build a school and learn more. They also began to plant a few crops to supplement their food supply obtained by hunting and fishing. In this way, a very effective and peaceful halt has been made to encroachment upon their lands by outsiders. Without doubt, the very lives of these indigenous pepole have been preserved as well. Hopefully, a repetition of tragic Native American history has been avoided. Cultural understanding is being fostered between the indigenous population and the colonists. The local people are learning to handle the accoutrements of civilization without negating their own values and, certainly, the colonists are viewing the indigenous people with a new and a profound respect.

Focus on Adults

While the system of bilingual-bicultural schooling is a tremendous boon to indigenous communities who wish to take a recognized place within a nation, it must be acknowledged that the principal focus of attention is on the community's children, leaving the adult members unable to participate fully in the learning process. Unless special care is taken to remedy this problem, the system eventually can act as a dividing wedge between generations.

Such division is not nearly so pronounced if the adult world can take an active role in producing its own literature. Involvement of the adult community in literature production alongside an educational program for the children is the backbone for reaching the ultimate goal of the community: literacy.

Printed Page Valued

It has long been the practice of developmental agencies to subsidize books for reading classes or for distribution within a newly literate community. When developmental agents later see torn pages used for everything from cigarette "rollers" to toilet paper, they are disappointed, disillusioned, and often disgusted with the society for its seeming lack of values. Either the subsidy—and consequently the flow of books—is cut off, or a campaign is launched "to teach these people how to care for books." The end result is the same for both activities: books still are not valued and reading does not become a part of community life.

In order to ensure a continued respect for the value of books, the content must be good. If what the book says is so meaningful to the reader/hearer that it touches something deep within the heart, that book is going to be given good care. It may become worn and ragged from use—but never from abuse.

Unity Promoted among Ethnic Entities

Several respondents noted that letter writing between villages had increased considerably, improving relationships within the language group. Obviously, the spread of good will depends on what message is carried in the letter. Nevertheless, access to written communication has thus far proved to be a plus in the matter of promoting good relationships and in bringing unity.

Through participation in multilanguage workshops, trainees from differing ethnic groups have gained mutual respect and camaraderie which is difficult to generate in other settings. The close association and new understanding of the role and value of each language often prove factors for unification rather than divisiveness among ethnic groups. Above all, having a common goal—literacy—promotes unity among those struggling to attain it.

Reading Ability among Semiliterates Advances

The educational picture among linguistic minorities in many countries indicates that semiliterates or neoliterates abound. Many children and young-to-middle-aged adults have attended school for one or two years and have learned to call out more or less correctly the sounds symbolized on a page, usually representing a language which is not their mother tongue. They pass the reading tests, and are counted as literates. But do they actually read? The percentage of those who continue reading, for pleasure or for profit, is usually very low.

Unesco's Julian Behrstock, speaking on the topic of "Books for All" before the Seventh IRA World Congress on Reading in 1978, stated that no less than 600 million Africans are classified as literate but, for the most part, these people are nonreaders. He related this condition to the source and content of reading material for Africa: 75 percent of their books come from Europe and deal with content of interest primarily to Europeans.

Such trends of dependence must be reversed if developing countries are to gain the status assigned to literate nations, a goal they desire and which they are fully capable of attaining. Utilizing local languages is one way the goal can be reached. Increasing amounts of literature written and produced locally greatly stimulate reading by the literate, but nonreading, members of a community.

Craving for Knowledge Awakened

In his autobiography (Little and Haley, 1965:179), Malcolm X stated that although his reading ability was extremely poor, having books to read while he was in prison somehow "awakened a long dormant craving to be mentally alive." This same deep desire has been noted among preliterate people as culturally relevant books in their language have become available to them. It is therefore important that a wide range of topics be treated as soon as possible, to give ample opportunity for such interests to be nurtured.

Provision Made for Recording Historical Events

Many preliterate groups have played a part in the development of their nation's history but neither they nor the nation's educated sector may be fully aware of the significance of the role the group has played. The uncovering of such stories can provide an invaluable source of information, adding to the store of historical data. Such chronicles, concerning local battles fought in Mexico's Revolution of 1910, were found among the Tzotzils of Mexico (see Wasserstrom, 1979). These accounts have made a significant contribution to younger generations by helping them understand that earlier era and the effect of the Revolution upon indigenous people. The older generation also benefited in that they understood for the first time that battles they witnessed as children were not just local fights with some invaders, but were actually part of a much larger whole that affected the nation.

An indigenous community may not immediately recognize all eight advantages mentioned in this section, but the acknowledgement of even a few of the foregoing can stimulate a community to unified action. And when that happens, the group is well on the way to self-perpetuating literacy.

From the Perspective of the Educator

Many of the respondents to my information-seeking letter linked materials produced by local authors with the bilingual-bicultural schools of the area. Primarily, they thought of the latter as producing future readers, thus creating a market for the materials written. Establishment of such a market is of vital importance if a program is to become self-propagating.

But what affect does locally produced reading material have on the pupils of these schools now—in the context of their years of study? Is their learning affected by the local literature? Is school work made easier, more interesting, more quickly utilized? Some respondents noted differences here, too.

Better Reading with More Materials

One respondent noted that aborigine children in an Australian bilingual school were heard to use a much more natural intonation in their reading with a smoother flow and phrasing, once both they and their parents had been exposed to reading materials written by peers. Previous observation in the school had shown them to be monotonous, word-by-word "encoders" of the sounds symbolized on the page. Nothing about their reading had shown them to be "decoders" of a message. An increase in locally authored materials is gradually changing the old patterns of meaningless or, at best, stilted reading.

Every experienced reading teacher recognizes the importance of adults reading to children in their preschool and primary school years. But how can this be done for children of a preliterate society unless a literature is somehow provided? Reading stories to children in a language they do not understand is a foolproof method for turning off the attention button. It is a signal to begin doing anything but listening. If this is the extent of their exposure to reading, it is no wonder children develop an automatic aversion to it, or consider it something unintelligible and alien.

In some bilingual schools, older children write stories for reading to younger children, a practice becoming popular in the United States. In Peru, one of the supervisors in a Quechua bilingual education system seized upon the idea of all the schools of his district sharing a simplified silk screen duplicator. He envisioned that each school would have it to use for a month or six weeks, for printing materials written by upper grade children. These materials would serve for supplementary reading in the same grade and in lower grades not only in that school but in all the other schools of the district. He thus visualized the building up of a library in each school in minimal time.

Depth to Bilingual Teacher Training

A weakness of many bilingual education training programs is that the teachers are given little opportunity to develop facility in handling their own language in writing. They are taught how to read and how to teach from a primer written in their mother tongue, but development of competency and ease in writing their language often is ignored. Consequently, their teaching becomes rote and then sterile. If the teacher is not shown how to become creative in this medium, it is guaranteed that the students will never become creative either. In fact, learners quickly pick up the idea that written works of the mother tongue are confined to the pages of their primers.

Recently the department of education in one of the Central American countries sent a group of bilingual teacher trainees to a one-week-writer-training session. It is encouraging to note that educational authorities are beginning to recognize this lack in the training program and are seeking to remedy it. (It will be even more encouraging when more than one week's worth of attention is paid to this area of a teacher's training.)

If educators are serious about the scholastic development of their students, they will welcome anything that enhances their teaching, anything that makes study more meaningful to their pupils. A community that embraces reading and writing as a part of its own sphere of intimate interest is one of the greatest boosts educators working in developing countries could possibly desire, if their work is to be of a lasting nature.

From the Perspective of the Field Linguist

Much of this section focuses on the needs of the SIL field linguist whose goals include activities that range from linguistic investigation to the translation of Scripture. Other field workers involved in a preliterate society also will find these thoughts applicable to their goals.

Discerning field linguists understand that self- perpetuating community literacy is basic to adoption of whatever innovation is desired by that community. Therefore, rather than allowing themselves to become preoccupied with a particular project, linguists will put community literacy at the top of a list of objectives for the early phases of the work. To reach this objective, a field linguist must realize that a community's introduction to reading is very important. The society must be able to identify with the reading material and to find it both meaningful and enjoyable. This is, however, only one part of the task facing field linguists working in a preliterate society; how to accomplish all the goals in a minimal amount of time is the ever present question.

One of the most frustrating factors imposed upon the linguist may be a limitation of time. Ten years may well be the maximum time allowable for what appears to be a monumental task: learning to speak an unwritten language and to operate within the societal borders; discovering and writing an intelligible display of the language's phonological, grammatical, and syntactic structures, establishing a core of literates from whom literacy and literature will spread; gathering and publishing a dictionary of several thousand entries (usually in two parts, cross-referencing both the local language and the national language); and carrying out the main humanitarian purpose for which the field person has chosen to become involved with that society in the first place. No matter what the ultimate objective, each aspect can loom as a major undertaking. Discouragement and bewilderment may beset the SIL field linguistic team who wonders how all this can possibly be done in only ten years. Thus it is of utmost importance that activities be planned and timed to accomplish several goals at once, in order to maximize the effectiveness of each.

Drawing from the questionnaire responses and other reports of field colleagues, this section will attempt to show how the training of local authors can facilitate and speed several vital phases of a field program.

Learning to Communicate

Obviously, a way of direct communication must be established early in a program. For field linguists this means learning to speak the language rather than relying on interpreters. Thus, communication is direct and much more satisfactory. (For detailed information on learning to speak an unwritten language, see Gudschinsky 1967, Healey 1975, Samarin 1967.) It is essential that field linguists plan sufficient time in their programs for adequate language investigation and learning so they can control the basic language patterns and can communicate on most topics before proceeding with a full program of literacy, teaching, or other community development projects.

Many of the respondents who had participated early in writer-training workshops, i.e. within the first two years of language work, indicated that in the process they saw their own proficiency in language use take a forward leap. The introduction to expressed thought patterning through such intensive work with a local author-in-training is unparalleled by other language learning activity.

One respondent found that a lot of time was saved in his language analysis and conversation-learning programs because the writer whom he had trained was then able to transcribe texts recorded on tape by other speakers. "He could hear what isn't there! That is, what is there syntactically, but not phonologically." The trainee, as a native speaker of the language, was able to expand the elided phonological forms or incomplete verbal expressions so the learner could make sense of the passage and become aware of the psycholinguistic rules of elision in that particular language.

Raymond L. Johnston (1977:12) observed:

It may even be the case that the more predictable the occurrence of some functional element in the grammar, the less necessary it is to say it, because it is in fact predictable from the grammatical context. However, in the written mode it will be painfully clear that something has been omitted.

It is only to the native speaker/reader that the omission of the grammatical element is clear. To a new language learner there is only distressing confusion.

Another highly important feature of learning the communication process is knowing the local culture and how to converse within its boundaries. Here, again, the materials produced by local authors provide for the field linguists the windows they need for observing and understanding the cultural features that open doors for entry into the society. Facility in cultural expression indicates that learners have "arrived" as speakers of the language fully as much as or more than their correct handling of the phonology or grammatical constructions of the language. Knowing the society, how to behave within its boundaries, what to talk about and how, are hallmarks of the individuals who have really learned.

Establishing an Orthography

Phonological analysis done early in the period of contact with a preliterate society enables the field linguist to make a tentative listing of orthographic symbols to serve as alphabet. (In most languages contacted thus far by SIL personnel, the Roman alphabet is used. Some few utilize other scripts.)

Initial choices of symbolization are just the beginning in the establishment of an alphabet. Selection of a final alphbet involves a host of other factors, some psycholinguistic in nature, others sociolinguistic. These cannot possibly be foreseen in their entirety by the field linguist who is not a native speaker of the language, and who is a relative newcomer.

While arbitrary decisions based upon linguistic study must be made in the initial and tentative selection of an orthography, the field linguists must steadfastly remind themselves that these choices are not necessarily the best, nor the final ones. Early attention to the training of writers often facilitates establishment of the orthography that will represent intuitive or psycholinguistic choice by speakers of the language, and their reaction to the sociological pressures for conformity (or nonconformity) to other alphabets in the area.

Natural process of selection arising from increased local production of reading material is demonstrated in the case of the Kura (Brazil). The need for a unified decision arose because at least three Kura speaking people were writing stories and other reading material, each one using an orthography which differed in some respects from the other two. A conference was subsequently arranged involving representatives of both local and national entities, but final decisions were made by the local group (Jones, 1978).

The problems of writing tone—i.e., whether it should be symbolized and, if so, how—often are settled through the increased production of reading materials at various levels. In this way, ample opportunity is given to observe reactions of both writers and readers, and the problems they may encounter. Orthographical changes can be made easily in the early stages of a literature program. If this natural testing period is ignored, field linguists run the risk of publishing much larger and very expensive works—Scriptures, dictionaries, translations of constitutional rights, manuals, histories—only to find that unwise choices of orthographic symbols form a major block for the readers. Perhaps the reason given by the frustrated reader may be no more than "The page looks funny with all those little marks under the vowels!" or "It should look more like such-and-such a language." Much time, grief, and money can be saved if these reactions are noted and satisfactory choices made long before larger works are undertaken.

Development of Linguistic Confidence

One of the most rewarding results of training writers is the freedom they develop in correcting the field linguist in verbal use or in the writing of language. Because the linguist operates in a world largely unknown to the preliterate person—the world of books, paper, writing, reading—a blind awe may develop in the minds of those to whom that world is a mystery, and they hesitate to offer correction to one considered so knowledgeable.

In recounting some of his language discoveries one SIL field linguist noted several times that his language helper had to "pluck up his courage" to offer suggestions as to how certain things should be written. One wonders how many errors in both speech and writing have gone uncorrected merely because language helpers were not courageous enough to suggest that something might be clearer if said differently.

However, once people are trained to write within their own linguistic and cultural frameworks, such inhibitions tend to disappear. One field linguist reported corrections in both pronunciation and writing taking place in this way:

> They often ask us, "How do *you* say this word?" as they point to something we have written. We answer with the word as we have learned to say it, whereupon they reply, "Wapishanas say it this way:_____." Or, they will ask another Wapishana speaker to say the word, and then gently ask us, "Shouldn't this have (e.g.) an *o* here?" (Dawson, 1978).

There is no better way to settle arguments (which can be endless and become very hot) among the field linguists concerning certain phonological problems than the opinion and proof offered by a native speaker of the language who is also a competent writer of the language. For example:

> For almost a year my husband and I had an argument about a pre-stop glottal which he swore was not there, or if it was heard at all, was subphonemic. This particular language has been written for a long time and two other SIL teams over a period of twenty years had never heard a pre-stop glottal. One day one of the new authors said to me, "Look, here's one thing your husband doesn't know yet." And he wrote two words showing a pre-stop glottal in contrastive environments. Also, other local authors have recently brought to our attention a word-initial glottal which we didn't know was phonemic . . . (Dooley, 1978).

The advisability of encouraging the development of local authors during the early stages of a program cannot be over-emphasized from the point of view of orthography establishment.

Accomplishment of Larger Goals Facilitated

Several indigenous writers are currently assisting in the preparation of larger, more exacting works. In several cases, writers are participating in the compilation of dictionary entries. From each account they write, they make a file slip for every word, giving a definition, an illustrative sentence, and the nearest equivalent in the national language. These slips will eventually form the bulk of dictionary entries, and the published volume will pay tribute to their work.

Several field linguists reported that writer-training had clearly indicated the choice of those people who had talent to do efficient translation of other work, and had rapidly brought them to the point where they could easily learn the principles of translation.

By far the most significant contribution of local authors to the field linguist's ultimate goal is that a way is prepared for an easy grasp of whatever innovation is to be introduced. If the goal is improvement of the soil, then the people are prepared to read instructions and act on them. If the goal is introduction of an industry, readers are equipped to handle much of what is entailed. If the goal is distribution of literature, readers are unhindered by perplexity or false notions regarding the function of "paper" and can go directly to content.

In short, a society which produces its own literature is prepared to meet an innovation on its own ground, because it shares with the innovators an understanding of that ground.

Summary

Even though we have not yet seen a whole society "turn literate" as a result of training local authors, there is sufficient evidence that these writers are making a sizable contribution toward such a day.

The benefits to the individual writer are many and vivid. The advantages to the community are similar to those for the writer, for it must be recognized that communities are made up of individuals acting as a unit. Self-esteem, assurance in the worth of the minority language, clarified understanding of the way of books, preservation of records of historical events and customs from the past, and preparation for handling conduct in a rapidly changing world, may make the difference between life and death for a people.

The educator will find that teaching the young is facilitated because reading for meaning has become a part of the whole community, and because the teachers are better prepared to handle the written mode of communication.

Field linguists find their work speeded at nearly every level, from learning to speak the language to selecting an orthography to compiling dictionary entries to translating a major work. Field workers who fail to consider the training of local authors early in their careers because of a desire to "go directly to the task" are prolonging the task and making it much more difficult than needed.

References

Behrstock, Julian. Books for all: International cooperation to promote reading. *Journal of Reading*, 1980, *23*, 313-319.
Dawson, Beverly. Personal communication. Suriname: Summer Institute of Linguistics, 1978.
Dooley, Kathie. Personal communication. Brazil: Summer Institute of Linguistics, 1978.
Gudschinsky, Sarah C. *How to learn an unwritten language*. New York: Holt, Rinehart and Winston, 1967.
Healey, Alan. *Language learner's field guide*. Ukarumpa, Papua New Guinea: Summer Institute of Linguistics, 1975.
Johnston, Raymond Leslie. Distinctive aspects of the syntax of written language in local languages of Papua New Guinea. Unpublished manuscript, 1977.

Jones, Joan. Kura (Bakairí) orthography conference: Growth in competence. *Notes on Literacy,* 1978, *24,* 1-8.

Keesing, Roger M., and Keesing, Felix M. *New perspectives in cultural anthropology.* New York: Holt, Rinehart and Winston, 1971.

Larson, Mildred L., Davis, Patricia M., and Davila, Marlene Ballena. *Educacon Bilingue: Una Experiencia en la Amazonia Peruana.* Lima, Peru: Editor/Ignacio Prado Pastor, 1979.

Little, Malcolm, with the assistance of Alex Haley. *The autobiography of Malcolm X.* New York: Grove Press, 1965.

Samarin, William J. *Field linguistics.* New York: Holt, Rinehart and Winston, 1967.

Wasserstrom, Robert. *En sus própias palabras.* México, D.F.; Centro Antropológico de Documentación Para América Latina. Instituto de Asesoría Antropológico Para la Región Maya, 1978.

"Xamanixna." *Tu Lichihuinan "Xamanixna" ó Narraciones de "El Sonador."* México, D.F.: Instituto Lingüístico de Verano en coordinación con la Secretaria de Educación Extraescolar en el Medio Indígena, 1974.

Chapter Six

Problems Pinpointed

Training indigenous authors as the key to bootstrap literacy has been presented as potentially sucessful. Reports of adoption and adaptation indicate that the idea has definite worth. However, the process is not without rather perplexing problems, solutions for which are being sought. In this chapter we will consider the problems which have surfaced through the responses to the 1977 questionnaire.

The problems center around one basic aspect of the overall goal: how to implement the continuance of literature production so that a preliterate society will truly be able to turn the corner into self-sustaining literacy. The following categories of problems will be considered: 1) engaging community support, 2) maintaining the flow of new materials, 3) duplicating or printing materials, and 4) distributing materials.

Pinpointing the problems is the first step toward discovery of solutions. In some cases, suggestions will be offered as to how the problem may be resolved. In other cases, allusion will be made to underlying questions such as: How has the problem been noted? Has the cultural value system been violated in some way? What attitudes or procedures indicate need for change, and on whose part? Are the measures to be taken preventative or remedial, and how can they be administered? Hopefully, as such questions are asked, solutions will present themselves and the problems will eventually disappear.

Soliciting and Ensuring Community Support

Usually if community leaders are approached early with the idea of self-help literature and literacy, and if the early training includes these leaders or their appointees, there is little problem in winning lasting support.

In some cases it may be extremely difficult to get community leaders personally involved at the onset, probably because they have different ideas as to the direction community life should take or because they are already involved in many time-consuming projects or because they have no notion that such writing can be done. In these cases it is wiser to concentrate on casual, informal training of various people over a period of time, exercising great care to keep community leaders informed as to what is taking place. Samples of stories produced should be made immediately available to "town hall" with a demonstration of how they can be read. Some SIL colleagues have found this to be a highly profitable procedure. They have been alert to making use of the sparks of interest shown by town officials, and to using that interest to get the officials involved in some way. Perhaps the mayor's own creative writing has been printed or the mayor has written an endorsement of others' writings. The mayor's approval has been incorporated in the printed booklet in the introduction or foreword.

After progress has been made in producing materials with some degree of community participation, the planning of a celebration which conforms to local standards for such occasions, and to which the whole community is invited, may prove to be well worth the expense and activity involved. Demonstrations of what can be done, how it is done, recognition of those who have done it, and display of the results, may prove to be not only the culmination of efforts but the incentive for others to participate in the next period of training and literature production. A community festival with emphasis upon production of reading materials may become an annual affair and, thus, a part of community life.

If possible, recognition by representatives of the national society should be part of the celebration. Their recognition and approval can do much toward establishing the importance of reading and writing in the minds of the preliterate people;

at the same time the dominant members of the society develop a new perspective about the capacities and capabilities of the minority group.

Maintaining the Flow of New Materials

The knottiest problem reported lies in the area of keeping writers producing when the workshop is over and they are back in the home environment. Even when the intended audience shows great interest in the materials, getting the writer to keep on writing without constant prodding by the field linguist may be difficult.

Several aspects of the problem will be discussed; preventative measures, field linguists' expectations (are they realistic?), instilling desirable attitudes toward writing, preference by readers for the field linguists' writings as opposed to those of the indigenous authors, and problems of teaching punctuation rules as a part of perfecting the writing. All of these affect the writers' continued production.

Harking back to the previous topic of community involvement, it is well to remind ourselves that preventative measures are better than remedial. The community needs to become involved from the beginning in the production of literature. Full involvement will come about only when a sizable proportion of the group becomes "hooked on books." With the demand will come the incentive to produce.

It is also good to examine our own attitudes about what is reasonable to expect with regard to ongoing production. It is easy to pin all our hopes and expectations on the trainees (perhaps on just one trainee) who have attended only one workshop. Or we may expect too much from one short training period, forgetting that the custom of centuries of living without books does not disappear easily. The realization of need does not develop overnight.

With regard to the writers themselves, has the habit of writing become established through one workshop experience? How can a favorable attitude be fostered until the habit is established? In training children to write, Sealey, Sealey, and Millmore (1979) say that the inculcation of an attitude that bids children to turn naturally to the written mode of expression is neither simple nor easy. They have found two main factors in helping writing to flourish: the personal satisfaction the child experiences in writing, and the response the writing evokes on the part of others. They also state that the best atmosphere for stimulating further writing seems to be "in classrooms where many activities are taking place which are largely self-generated and are accompanied by a great deal of purposeful discussion about the work in hand" (Sealey, et al., 1979:3).

Personal satisfaction has been found to be a highly motivating force in keeping indigenous writers at the job. One field linguist left her typewriter in the care of an older man who had participated in a workshop where he had learned to type his stories. When she returned after a three-month absence, she found a stack of pages he has written—merely because he wanted to.

Another field linguist found that a former trainee, entirely on his own initiative, had made a calendar, laboriously drawing the squares, numbering them accurately for each month, and then illustrating each month with appropriate sesasonal pictures from the area. He had then prepared stencils and had run off twenty copies of the calendar on the silk-screen duplicator.

In both cases, the motivation was simply that the men were fascinated by what they had discovered they could do, and they wanted to keep on doing it.

But personal satisfaction alone has its limitations. It is the response that the writing evokes on the part of others that keeps writers at the job when their own satisfaction has been fulfilled. It has been said that creativity is often sparked by the influence or suggestion of others. It this is true in Western society, how much truer it is in a society which has found that its survival depends on the cooperation and unity of its members. If the community really wants to produce written materials, ways will be found to do it, no matter what the difficulties.

It should be recognized by field linguists or trainers that their responsibilities for encouraging writers does not end with the closing program of the first workshop. There is a responsibility to ease the writer's transition into the home environment, to encourage recognition by the community, and to help plan other workshops or training courses to increase the number of contributors to an ongoing program. It is rare that such a program gets seriously underway with just one individual writer who has had a three to six week training course. A devastating feeling of isolation can come to a writer who is the only one in the community trained to write. It is very difficult to keep up the momentum when one operates alone, especially in a society which is geared toward group activity, and which is *not* used to having a flow of reading material.

Writers' clubs may serve to provide companionship and a stimulus for continued production, especially if the club works on a series of special projects, such as a periodical or a newssheet. In Guatemala, the Quiché and Cakchiquel trainees have formed two writers' clubs and it appears that the momentum built up by the workshops will continue to push production. A field linguist who is currently acting as advisor to the Quiché group has found far less to do than at first anticipated. Several writers are involved in the club—enough to carry the newssheet project along very well—and enthusiasm is high. An ongoing program appears likely, for many other Quiché people are clamoring for the training. They all want to be involved.

Another facet of the problem of ongoing literature reported by a few of the respondents to the questionnaire is that "native-authored materials just do not work. People prefer materials that the field linguists have written." It is extremely difficult from a remote position to evaluate such statements. However, the following suggestions may have some bearing on this problem.

Sometimes a group is so motivated for inclusion into the national language and culture that they cannot accept any program that does not immediately produce their desired objective. In such cases, these desires should certainly be taken into account and provision made for some sort of fulfillment. If the field linguist finds a high degree of bilingualism, it may be that materials exclusively in the national language may be indicated, at least at the beginning. Diglot materials, with the two languages given equal focus, may follow.

In other cases, it may be that the field linguist made only a halfhearted attempt to train writers. Perhaps those who were trained were not those who were really talented for this type of work. An indigenous society is like any other in that there is found a diversity of talent. Not all people in our society possess the same talents, and neither do all people in theirs. Field linguists must then look further, all the while making sure they are establishing a proper atmosphere where writers can develop and where there is plenty of opportunity for them to do so. The "Pygmalion principle" (Rosenthal, 1968) or the self-fulfilling prophecy is at work here. If linguists are convinced that no writers will ever develop in a particular society, it is highly likely they will be proven correct.

As outsiders from so-called "developed countries," we must be mindful that we are programed to consider that training at the university-and-beyond levels has fitted us for doing the work better than the preliterate-just-turning-literate. And we may be right. Perhaps we *can* state simple experiences in better order or more succinctly than can the first writer trainee, even in a language not our own. But while our doing the writing may satisfy our egos and give opportunity to fulfill our *raison d'etre*, the question remains: how will this society become truly literate if it must depend on the outsider for its reading material?

My advice comes too late to be of help to those who have already encountered this problem, for it is this: *Never allow the community the option of choosing between the writings of the indigenous authors and those of the outsider.* In other words, we must put out of our minds the possibility of our producing creatively written material in their language. The decision, perhaps, will be made on the altar of sacrifice with "ego" as the burnt offering to the gods-of-final-objectives. But the decision must, nevertheless, be made.

Teaching punctuation rules was listed by several respondents as a major hurdle in bringing trainees into independent writing. They reported having to spend an inordinate amount of time trying to teach the use of commas, semicolons, and quotation and question marks. In general, the concept of punctuation seemed to be too difficult for many of the trainees to grasp.

Two comments are in order here. One is in the form of a question: Is the field worker fully cognizant of the language's grammatical bits that function on the discourse level? These bits may be actual words or morphemes that in themselves indicate questions, exclamations, or quotations. Their usage may do the same for that particular stream of speech that intonation does for English. Simply stated, punctuation marks are the written forms developed to tell the reader what intonation (and thus meaning) is intended by the writer.

One field linguist, well aware of the true function of punctuation, reported that she delayed teaching any punctuation whatsoever until the new readers encountered difficulties in reading because they had no clues as to the intonation and meaning their peer author wanted to convey. Only at that point was punctuation introduced into the writing. Readers and writers then caught on quickly to the reasons for and the forms of punctuation and were able to proceed without further problems. This type of delayed attack on the question is strongly advocated.

The second comment is in the form of an admonition: We should not look for perfection too soon. Field workers may be too well oriented to the goal of perfection. They desire that the expressions be just right and that the overall page appearance be faultless. If the material looks otherwise, it is reworked until the indigenous author scarcely recognizes that he or she has had any part in it. This is deadly. The end result may be a technically correct book—and a completely discouraged author who will never write anything again. Preoccupation of the trainer with the details of complete sentences or sentences with proper punctuation can kill creativity before it is born.

Rather, emphasis should be placed on lucid, interesting verbal expression, with as clear representation on the page as the trainee is capable of doing at that time. The final judgment should be the collective opinion of those who read and the trainee should be taught to look for these opinions, to listen to them, and to remedy the work accordingly.

Careful attention should be paid to the plea expressed by Godfried Bamfo, a Ghanaian educator, speaking to a congress of West Africans and missionaries assembled to discuss the matter of books for West Africans. He said:

> It is well known that many expatriate missionary personnel did not come to Africa with great qualifications

in their field of work, nor even a previous experience in that field of work. They came to Africa, and just tried. With their own basic education, they trusted the Lord, and learnt through their mistakes. Give us Africans the same opportunity, if you have really come to help us (Bamfo, 1972:11).

Problems of Printing/Duplicating

The high cost of book production is a serious problem. Even the simplest procedures sometimes involve expenditures almost impossible for an indigenous community. Stencils, ink, and the cheapest kind of paper (newsprint) are items that must be imported by many of the developing countries. Furthermore, an import duty is often imposed making it even more difficult for the country to advance in the area where it most wants to advance—education. Mimeographs and typewriters are also extremely high priced since they, too, must be imported. However, some groups in West Africa have become so excited about doing their own printing that they have banded together and purchased equipment. A mimeograph was purchased by one church congregation even before anyone in the group knew how to operate it or had written anything to be duplicated.

Good success is found with the small, hand-operated, one-page-at-a-time, silk-screen duplicator. These are available commercially in some countries, and can also be built at a minimal cost by anyone with even a rudimentary knowledge of carpentry (see Appendix C for instructions). Even though this type of duplicator can make an enormous reduction in the cost of local printing, problems are nevertheless encountered. Procurement of a silk-like material that is strong, yet thin enough to allow an even spread of a small amount of ink is difficult in many countries. The high price of paper, stencils, and ink is still a nearly insurmountable problem for many preliterate societies, especially for those living in very remote areas.

Perhaps this problem should be tackled on levels of society other than the local community. Here a sponsoring body of national educators and legislators may become involved. Is it too much to suppose that laws could be either changed or enacted, as the case may be, to allow duty-free importation of paper? Or that business personnel could be persuaded that a sufficient market can be built up so that a paper mill would be profitable? Developing countries which are serious about the problem of illiteracy among their peoples should recognize that laws which inhibit the procurement of materials are in direct counteraction to the fulfillment of their desires for progress. True, this is an area to be handled by national leaders. Responsibility on the local level is to make the national leaders aware of the growing interests and abilities on the village levels, especially among the minority language groups.

A related problem lies in the area of the source of funding. Some indigenous societies frown upon the idea of one person's making a profit by selling anything to fellow group members. One shares what one has by giving it, not by selling it. This presents acute problems to writers who have produced their own materials and must replace at least what has been spent if more is to be produced.

The usual reaction to this problem by the field linguist is simple: Find outside funding in the form of grants, gifts, or personal savings. It could be that at least partial help in initial stages of a literature-production program should be considered. However, the question must still be asked: *Will outside funding result in ongoing literacy for the minority group?* Unfortunately, this question is seldom asked in time to forestall negative effects. Only when some form of cooperative provision is made to which both the outside funding agency and the local community are in agreement and which they are prepared to carry out, will there be a chance that the ultimate goal can be reached with outside assistance.

Again, a major part of the answer to this problem lies in community involvement in the literature-production project from the earliest stages possible, with everyone contributing to the production and sharing the results. This means that everyone must be in favor of the project.

Remoteness of location of the minority group may present problems in the procurement of materials from urban centers. Reports from Colombia and Brazil indicate there are many groups whose writers have to travel several days by canoe or by foot in order to contact the closest source of supply of paper and ink. It has been suggested that nationals sympathetic to the goals of the minority groups could be pressed into service to facilitate the procurement of materials. This is a very real possibility and should be explored. It must be pointed out, however, that nationals who have not had long-term contact with indigenous groups must be trained as much as any other outsiders concerning the indigenous thought patterns and ways of operating. Otherwise, it is too easy for old patterns of paternalism or even of hostility to rear their heads.

Storage problems in some climates present major difficulties. Mildew and termites can quickly destroy a stack of booklets waiting to be distributed. It may be that a village "library" should not be a shelf nor a building but an airtight metal box (Cates, 1970), and that the quantity ordered should be limited to the number of metal boxes distributed throughout a particular language area. Innovative ideas must be sought and put to work in an effort to find solutions appropriate to the exigencies of the situation.

Distribution of Materials

One field team reported a happy arrangement in Nigeria where a local bookshop was eager to carry all kinds of reading material in the local language. The shop owners even financed the printing of the books. Unfortunately, this kind of situation is rare. By far the majority of respondents noted difficulties in fostering distribution of newly printed materials throughout a community and into neighboring towns and villages. Finding distributors who want to sell, who know how to sell, and who enjoy selling are reported to be the main problems in sustaining a market. Most of these respondents noted that they, themselves, have to sell the books. On the positive side, this function has enabled some field linguists to enter into community life in a way that is acceptable and understandable to the local group.

For the most part, however, field workers who are the booksellers are not the ones who have taken seriously the idea of training indigenous authors and book producers. They began the task of selling books several years ago and have developed a system and technique which villagers may hesitate to try to copy. This is the foreigner's role, it carries prestige, and community members steer clear of intruding upon it. The pattern has been established and daily becomes more difficult to break.

The overriding question which must be settled is this: Is distribution of reading material a part of bootstrap literacy? To me, it is a very important part. If a preliterate society is to become literate largely through its own effort, its involvement in distributing books is vital. Early participation by the whole community in writing and producing newssheets or booklets should lead naturally to community participation in distribution.

In those societies where sales (rather than making gifts to all one's friends and relatives) are permissible, the following questions may act as guidelines in finding booksellers:

- How is selling done ordinarily in this community? Door-to-door? In homes? In shops?
- Who does the selling of which things?
- What is the usual percentage of profit made from sales in local stores?
- Have arrangements been made so that book sales will be profitable to the seller?
- Do the sellers know how to read well, so they can give convincing demonstrations of the product?
- Do the sellers know how to display books so that customers will be likely to see them and decide whether to buy?
- Is there a sufficient variety of themes in the display so that buyers will have a choice?
- Does the material content reflect the interests of the community, or is it mainly on topics which the field linguist thinks the community should know about?

In discussions with field linguists, I have discovered that they inadvertently force their choices of subject material upon the writers. They have not consciously done so; but a frown, a hesitation to accept certain material contrasted with overwhelming enthusiasm for other kinds of material, are easily interpreted as a strong disapproval or approval. Thus, the tone is set by the outsider instead of by the indigenous writer or the minority group.

Recently a field linguist confided his disappointment in the community's waning interest in buying a certain newssheet, largely the work of one indigenous writer-typist-printer who had long been in close association with field linguists and with others of a nonindigenous society. The person was an efficient writer, but nobody was reading.

Questioning revealed that only one item of Stage I character appeared regularly in the newspaper—a riddle. Once people had flipped the pages to find the riddle, their interest in reading the rest of the paper disappeared. Other topics included national history, geography of the country, descriptions of animals found in the zoo, and lessons to teach the national language. Looking over this list, it is easy to see that the riddle was the only item that clearly spoke of the community's life. While the other topics could well hold much interest for some groups, it is evident that for this group they could not. I am forced to conclude that the choice of reading material had definitely been influenced by outside forces, and the regular inclusion of these topics had killed the possibility of other writers becoming involved in the newspaper.

This question of the outsider's influence as to topic is closely akin to another, concerning morality or the lack of it, as depicted in some writings. Often the material is judged according to the field linguist's standard, not by what the society considers to be suitable for printing. The question is a delicate one, demanding great sensitivity. The safest procedure is to make sure that the community leadership takes responsibility for making a decision. Removing themselves from such decision-making can be very difficult for the field linguists, but it must be done. In the workshops which I have held, certain principles such as accuracy of information, appropriateness of material for publication, and the nature of "permanency" of written material are thoroughly discussed in the courses, so that writer-trainees may early become well aware of foreseeable problems and how to avoid them. But final decisions must rest with the community leadership, not with the field linguist.

Summary

Bootstrap literature is not initiated easily without wise counsel and some action by the catalyst. Knowing how much action to take or not to take characterizes the wise counselor. Problems are bound to turn up during the process and their early recognition is the first step toward solving them.

In this chapter we have discussed the problems relating to securing community support and cooperation, to maintaining a continuing flow of literature, to printing, and to distributing materials. For the most part, taking care of the first problem—engaging community support—will do much toward alleviating the other three.

References

Bamfo, Godfried. Missions and Africanization. In *Winning West Africa with books*. Ghana: Evangelical Literature Fellowship of West Africa in association with Asempa Publishers, 1972.

Cates, Ann Roke. Village libraries. *Read*, 1970, 5, 24-26.

Rosenthal, Robert, and Jacobson, Lenore. *Pygmalion in the classroom*. New York: Holt, Rinehart and Winston, 1968.

Sealey, Leonard, Sealey, Nancy, and Fillmore, Marcia. *Children's writing: An approach for the primary grades*. Newark, Delaware: International Reading Association, 1979.

Part Two

How to Conduct
a Writer Training Workshop

Chapter Seven

Preworkshop Planning and Preparation

If a workshop appears to be smooth running, with a high degree of active and successful participation by everyone involved, it means that a great deal of planning, preparation, and dissemination of information took place long before the workshop began. Six months to a year ahead of the course's opening date is not too early to begin planning for a workshop. The earlier the participants are aware of what will be involved, the greater will be their own psychological preparation, the more successful will be their work, and the more they will enjoy it.

This chapter deals with various aspects of the workshop planning phase, presented as follows:

> Type of workshop
> > Single language or multilanguage?
> > Location
>
> Participants
> > Sponsoring field linguists
> > Writer-trainees
>
> Advance information
> > To field linguists and trainees
> > To interested members of the dominant society
>
> Teaching personnel
> > Director
> > Consultants
> > Guidelines for consultants
>
> Logistics checklist

Type of Workshop
Single Language or Multilanguage?

Location

Reports from the fourteen countries in which the Summer
Institute of Linguistics has sponsored indigenous author-
training workshops show that the most common type of workshop has been the multilanguage rather than single language.
Several reasons for this choice come to mind, the foremost
being that SIL linguists had already established a program of
getting together for multilanguage linguistic analysis and
translation workshops, where they and their indigenous
coworkers tackled linguistic or translation problems with the
help of special consultants. Following this multilanguage
pattern, the 1970 Mexico indigenous literature production
workshop dealt with eight languages with only one trainee
from each language.

In recent years, as field workers have given more serious
thought to the ultimate goal of an ongoing, indigenous program
of literacy, there has sprung up a growing concern for intensive
training of several writers from the same language group.
It has been recognized that a community is more likely to give
momentum to the innovation of a literature program if many of
its members, rather than just one or two, are involved in the
training. The exact number of single language workshops
under SIL sponsorship has not been officially reported, but
it is likely that at least a dozen have been conducted.

An SIL colleague in Brazil has had experience in both
multilanguage and single language workshops. The multilanguage courses were all held at a study center operated by
the SIL, and the single language courses were held in individual, local communities where each of those languages was
dominant. The following sums up her views concerning advantages and disadvantages of the two kinds of workshops
(Crofts, 1978).

Advantages of single language workshops
held in the local community

a.   Stimulation of innovation
      Since bookmaking supplies may not be easily
      available, adaptation and innovation are necessarily

built into the course, becoming valuable teaching elements. If the course is held in or near an urban area, there is a tendency to go to a supply store and buy whatever is needed. If the workshop is held in the local community, where supplies are normally unavailable, then both trainers and trainees are forced to search out other ways of attaining the desired objectives.

b. More complete training

Trainees tend to carry more responsibility if they are trained locally, learning to do many of the tasks that the linguists take care of when the workshop is held at an outside site or SIL center of operations. This includes operating a mimeograph, collating pages, and stapling or sewing booklets.

c. Reduction of culture adjustment problems

Trainees are happier because they do not have to adjust to strange living conditions and different foods. There is no homesickness among the trainees because there is no need to leave home while attending the course. Sponsoring linguists are relieved of great responsibility in that they are not obligated to pilot the trainees through the maze of an unfamiliar culture.

d. Smaller expense

Since transportation costs of the trainees are virtually eliminated, much less money need be spent on the training course. It must be remembered, however, that basic workshop supplies must be brought in, thereby increasing other costs.

e. Greater ease in demonstrating community involvement

Resources for story material are easily available, especially for those of Stage I variety. Thus it is easier to convey the idea of total community involvement as many other people, especially the older ones, see that they too can have a share in the production of reading material by contributing stories from their experiences, recounting folktales, and the like.

f. Built-in testing ground

Faster feedback on the materials produced may be obtained locally because the audience is right at hand.

There may be a delay of several weeks in getting such feedback when the materials are printed commercially, away from the local area.

g.   Direct teaching input
        Sharing one's work with one's peers is much easier in a single language workshop, whereas it must be translated into a common language in a multilanguage workshop. Much of the flavor can be lost in a translation, making it more difficult for the hearer to comment or to give helpful criticism. Although it has been feared that trainees may hesitate to have their writings read aloud to fellow students lest criticism be forthcoming, reports indicate that such fear is groundless. Instead, trainees enjoy having others read their work and they look forward eagerly to the reactions of the readers (or hearers, if the story is read to them) and to their ensuing commentary.

While the above points are completely valid, Crofts is of two minds on the subject of single language versus multilanguage workshops. She has discovered that taking trainees to a central location for training in company with those speaking other indigenous languages, may be of even more benefit.

Advantages of multilanguage workshops held outside the local environment

a.   Social enrichment
        The intergroup encounter is an enriching experience in that thought processes are stimulated by the cross-cultural contact. Actual shoulder-rubbing with others of different cultural backgrounds often has a bracing effect, especially when done in an amicable atmosphere where no one culture dominates.

b.   Faster development of esprit de corps
        It is easier to form a group consciousness because all activities are group-centered—housing, meals, socials, classes, and projects. It is more difficult to form this consciousness in the local setting where everyone goes home every afternoon. Evening programs of sports or socials are usually as helpful as classes in providing

the affective atmosphere essential in writer-training. These events may be difficult to arrange locally.

c. Exposure to a new world
     Horizons are expanded very rapidly because there are new and different things to see and do. This is especially true if the course is held in a semiurban area. Thus, much learning takes place in a way that would be impossible to foster in the local community, and the trainees' writing may manifest a wider perspective.

d. Easy access to supplies
     Supplies are procured more easily, more economically, and more rapidly since the site is closer to stores and warehouses.

e. Easier demonstration to the official/national world
     Building and controlling an atmosphere of respect for both the language and the person appear easier near larger population centers. For the continuation of an indigenous language program it is important to win the approval and respect of members of the dominant society. These are more easily obtained if the workshop is held in a place that has easy access for educators and government officials, who often are willing to attend opening and closing ceremonies if minimal time has to be spent in getting to them. The presentation of work done by several different linguistic groups may be much more impressive to such officials than the work of just one group. Seeing the trainees in person and their obvious interest and pride in what they are accomplishing is much more impressive than being presented a stack of booklets with merely a verbal description of how they were produced.

f. Greater validity assigned to the training course by the community
     In the United States, "going away to school" somehow conveys greater prestige and value for college students than attending the local university while living at home. The same sentiment often prevails in an indigenous community. A training course held in a pres-

tige-carrying center may be considered much more valuable than the same course held in the local community.

Thus we see that there are advantages to both kinds of workshops: the single language held in the local community and the multilanguage held at a more central, semiurban location. Each project must be evaluated for its own sociological, economic, and physical needs.

Possibly the ideal is to initiate the idea and the process locally and expect participation later on in a larger training course held outside the group's area. This would be especially advantageous for groups having little access to well-populated centers of commerce or trade. Anticipation of later attending a more intensive training course could well be an incentive in itself in beginning stages, and might prove to be a helpful stimulus to apathetic communities that are hesitant to believe they are able to control their own future literacy.

The following discussion concerns a multilanguage workshop, held in a central location away from the local area.

Participants

Sponsoring Field Linguists

Since the field linguists play a vital role in any indigenous program of literature development, it is important that they be deeply involved in each training program. Often special seminars are held specifically to help the field linguists gain an in-depth understanding of the workshop goals and how these goals can contribute to the general literacy improvement goals of the groups with which they work.

The field linguists will, therefore, want to assist the trainees in every way possible, keeping alert to any problem that may be encountered. New teaching and new techniques may need to be clarified for the trainees by "their" linguists in separate teaching sessions in their own languages. The less the trainees control the national language, the more time the field linguists must devote to helping them.

Because the trainees are the focus of attention in a writer-training workshop, it may be tempting to the field linguists to plan to engage in other activity or study during the workshop time. However, the help, interest, and encouragement that they alone can give are crucial elements in the training of the indigenous writer. If the field linguists are obviously absorbed in other work, they may prove to be deterrents to, rather than stimulators of, rapid progress by the trainees, who often interpret the lack of help as a lack of interest or even as an opinion that the trainees' writing is unimportant.

Writer-trainees

The choice or selection of trainees has already been discussed. Here it is sufficient to say that the trainees occupy the limelight during the workshop. They are the object of attention for development in the field of literature production. All activities should be geared toward this development and toward the eventual goal of local production of written material.

Accommodations, companionship, food, activity, and recreation must all be of the type that is going to make for freedom of spirit and confidence that will allow maximum creativity for writing. One workshop report commented on the basement-type accommodations given to the trainees as being not only unfamiliar to the trainees, but even frightening. The report quoted one writer-trainee: "I saw a house under the ground. When I saw it I was frightened . . . . 'How will I get out again?' I said to myself . . . ."

It is true that we often find ourselves having to make do with less than ideal circumstances; however, situations such as the above would at least call for sympathetic understanding of the trainee's perspective, with explanation as to how to adjust to the problem if remediation really is impossible.

Advance information

To field linguists and trainees

Preliminary information may be sent to the field linguists in advance so they will know the exact nature of the workshop and what to expect from it. A letter such as the following (Murphy, 1977) will do much to set the mood for an upcoming workshop, and will enable everyone to achieve goals much more rapidly when the course gets underway.

Conducting a Writer Training Workshop

Purpose. The main purpose of the workshop is to produce indigenous-authored literature. There is solid theory behind the fact that locally authored material is naturally easier for the indigenous people to read. The authors know their own people best, can express themselves in completely cultural ways . . . and must know better than any outsider what will appeal to the local readers. In this situation, the author is the authority. Another purpose of the workshop is to stimulate pride in the culture and the language of each group.

Role-switch. In other workshop situations (e.g. linguistic or translation) the field linguist is in focus, but in this workshop the roles are reversed. The writer-trainee is in the focus and the field linguist becomes the helper.

Method. Three days a week the trainees will receive an hour's orientation designed to guide them gently toward the goal of writing for their people "back home." We attempt to stimulate creative thinking and widen their intellectual horizons, but we try not to structure them. Each culture is different and what motivates one may not motivate another. We trust that the trainees will develop group spirit and real friendships across tribal boundaries. Each day the trainees will have a typing class. Later they will learn to operate the spirit duplicators and other equipment necessary for final production of books.

Outings. Since many groups are interested in learning about the city, we arrange outings for them. These are learning experiences as well as enjoyable and entertaining diversion for the trainees, and they often want to write about these excursions.

WAYS IN WHICH YOU CAN BE INVOLVED

Hobbies. If you have any hobby which the trainees could see in action—e.g., model airplanes—please let us know so you may have a chance to share your interest with them.

Slides. We usually have a slide presentation each Saturday evening in which trainees present their home areas. If you have a set of slides, please consider helping one of the trainees whom you sponsor to show them. Or if you have a set of slides on any other subject, please consider showing them.

Games. Jigsaw puzzles, educational type games, and fun games are enjoyable to the trainees. Perhaps you would like to invite some of the trainees into your home to spend an evening playing some of these games.

Meals. Probably you will want to invite some trainees to a meal from time to time.

Ideas. Feel free to share any ideas you have to other ways to make this six weeks a great time for all concerned.

Similar information is sent to others who expect to be present at the study center. Thus, everyone is given an opportunity to understand the unique nature of the workshop. Through advance information, a spirit of cooperation is engendered from the beginning on various levels of activity.

To Interested Members of the Dominant Society

Attention and information are also given by Murphy to interested individuals of the dominant society through a brief, popular written article in the national language, published in a monthly newsletter by the local SIL office.

In at least one case, advisement to the larger society concerning an upcoming workshop proved to be detrimental to the workshop's objectives. Because of heavy press coverage before the beginning of the program, all the townspeople were aware of the influx of indigenous pepole into their midst, with the purpose of receiving training as writers in the various indigenous languages. The first excursion of the trainees to the city market turned into something of a nightmare for the budding authors, for they became objects of curiosity to everyone within sight. All strained to get a glimpse of the "Indians who were writing books." The trainees were embarrased at being pointed out; indeed, they could hardly move from one market stall to another so great was the crowd of curious townspeople. They were glad when the trip was cut short and they could escape the stares and questions. Consequently, the point of the assignment—to describe something of interest in the market—was completely lost.

Teaching Personnel

The teaching staff at an SIL workshop usually consists of a director and a corps of consultants.

The director is responsible for keeping in view the overall philosophy, structure, and goals of the workshop and for participating in the actual teaching as much as is feasible.

The consultants are responsible for the individual trainees and their development as writers. Often they deal directly with the trainees assigned to them. If the language barrier makes direct communication impossible, however, the consultants are more likely to deal with the field linguists who in turn work with the indigenous trainees under their sponsorship. Consultants also participate in teaching classes and in carrying out other activities as time and talent allow.

The roles of director and consultants are discussed below in more detail.

Director

Usually this role is filled by someone who has had previous firsthand experience in earlier workshops either as a sponsoring linguist or as a consultant-in-training. She/he has had opportunities to observe and to be involved without having carried full responsibility for a workshop. Such previous experience is not an absolute prerequisite; the individual's natural ability, creativity, and resourcefulness coupled with grassroots experience of interaction with indigenous people are the prime requisites. Previous training is helpful, however, especially from the point of view of gaining a perspective on the ultimate goal of an ongoing indigenous literature program.

It is often assumed that directors of writer-training workshops must be writers with sizable lists of books or articles to their credit. This is not necessarily true. While an impressive bibliography in English (or whatever is the director's first language) may possibly be an advantage to a director of an indigenous writer-training workshop, it certainly is not a prerequisite. The principal role of director lies somewhere between that of manager and psychologist-anthropologist who has had much experience in living with and learning the indigene's way of thinking. Above all, the director needs to see beyond the conventional or traditional way of doing things, and to be fearless in attempting innovation. A sense of what is practical for the situation at hand will provide needed balance.

The director should also have a clear understanding of the importance of the principle of "affect." Attention paid to attitudinal and personality factors in the teaching of reading has won recognition by educators as being as vital as the attention paid to linguistic and cognitive factors (see Athey, 1976). Close attention to these affective factors in training writers from preliterate cultures is just as important as it is in teaching reading to pupils of any culture. Setting an atmosphere in which focus is placed on the trainees to make them feel appreciated and comfortable yet challenged to produce their best is probably the chief ingredient of a successful workshop.

Qualities of such nature in a director may contribute far more to the development of successful indigenous writers than the director's competence in using techniques of writing in a major language. It is possible that extensive writing experience may be a detriment in a course of this kind. It could exert an unconscious pressure to structure the training along lines which make for good writing in the director's language but which may violate the rules of the indigenous language concerning thought pattern, sentence structure, and sequence of ideas or the sense of the serious, the esthetic, and the humorous.

Consultants

In addition to the obvious purpose of the consultant role, i.e., enabling trainees to reach their maximum production in the training period, each consultant also receives valuable training by carrying responsibility for various activities, such as: planning socials and sports, organizing excursions, preparing special projects and demonstrations, teaching classes in typing, teaching the preparation of copy for duplication, teaching the operation and care of duplicating equipment, teaching art classes, and teaching classes in language structure (phonology, grammar).

By participating in many aspects of a workshop, consultants are prepared to carry greater responsibilities in other courses later.

In some workshops there have been very few appointed consultants because of personnel shortage. However, participating field linguists have volunteered to help in various tasks. Such an arrangement may be quite advantageous since the field linguists thus become better prepared to conduct training sessions in the local villages.

Guidelines for Consultants

A consultant may find it useful to look for certain points when checking over a trainee's written material. The following have been outlined by Murphy (1977) as useful in guiding new consultants in workshops held in Brazil.

Audience
Does the writer really have other members of the society in mind as he/she writes? If Stage 1 material is too explicit it may indicate that the author in reality thinks of the consultant, rather than the home constituency, as audience. (Stages are described in Chapter 2.)

Accuracy
Are all the names and events accurate? Have any facts been misconstrued in any way?

Pronominal Reference
Are these references as clear in written style as in oral? Are there places where the characters should be specifically identified in a written account as to whether they are subject or object? Will another speaker-reader of the language understand the references without having to ask questions of the author?

Completeness
Are all pertinent phases of the action included? In a how-to-do-it, are all the steps included and are they in the right order?

Derogatory Statements
Does the author really want to express derogatory opinions in writing? Who might be hurt the most? Does the author understand all facets of the problem?

Time Sequence

Do the tenses switch from present to past and back again? Is this style natural to the language?

Implicitness

Is new terminology (e.g., elevator, traffic light, train) explained clearly? Have words borrowed from other languages been used without sufficient explanation for the uninitiated?

New Ideas

Have new situations been described with sufficient detail so that the reader (who has not seen or experienced them) will understand clearly? For example, is it clear that the exotic wild animals seen in the zoo are confined in cages, not running loose in the park where people are walking about? Are expressions too generalized, as: "They sell *everything* in the market . . . ." or "We went to see *this man* . . . ."

The consultant should remember that the above are guidelines only, and should not feel obligated to adhere to them rigidly.

A good consultant is one who develops the trainee's abilities. Emphasis is on the person and on the work produced. Care should be taken that suggestion for change or improvement of the work be interpreted as suggestion alone, and not as law. Final decisions must be made by the writer-trainee.

The consultant should seek to become aware of any problems of living accommodations, food, health, or anything else that may bother the trainee, and, therefore, hinder progress.

It is helpful for the consultant if each field linguist keeps a diary-type account of work sessions with the trainee, noting especially what training devices, advice, and suggestions are useful or not useful. This record can be of assistance to the consultant in working out techniques best suited to the trainee's capabilities.

Logistics Checklist

Georgia Hunter of the Mexico Branch of the Summer Institute of Linguistics has noted the following items as reminders of workshop logistics:

Accommodations
Housing
Study facilities
Seminar classrooms—chalkboards, etc.
Laundry, mail, buying of supplies

Writer-Trainees
Housing (if different from that of field linguists, e.g., families vs. singles)
Meals (place, adequacy, cost, etc.)
Laundry
Health needs
Restrictions (for reasons of safety)

Library Facilities (place, rules, hours)
Collection and cataloging of appropriate materials, if library is not already equipped
Library for sponsoring field linguists (technical, theoretical books)
Writer-trainee library
System for retrieval and return of materials borrowed, at end of workshop

Meetings (place, time, equipment needed)
Seminars
Writers' classes
Socials

Maintenance
Classrooms
Public restrooms
Writer-trainee rooms
General clean-up at end of workshop

Transportation
Availability of public vehicles

Social Activities
Planned socials or parties for writer-trainees
National holidays which may occur during workshop period
Equipment needed (projector(s), screen, tape recorders)

Publishing Standards or Requirements
Standards re content defined

Standards and checking procedures for any publication in national language

Format specifications

File copies (number, distribution)

Duplication Equipment
Person(s) responsible (for making equipment available, for repairing or demonstrating it)

Rules concerning use

Location

Method of charging for use

Availability and cost of paper, coverstock, ink, stencils

Typewriters and instruction books or lessons

Local Places of Interest for Trainee Excursions
Location

Transportation

Person(s) to contact

Hours

Cost

Time necessary for travel to and from

Value of experience

Background explanation (to make experience more meaningful to the trainees)

Accounting
Funding determined

Assignment of one person responsible for workshop bookkeeping

System outlined

Reports
To appropriate government agencies (e.g., a Brazilian government agency required weekly progress reports for each trainee, with samples of cursive writing, artwork, etc.)

General summary of workshop at the end (dates, participants, activities, topics discussed, outlines of lectures given, consulting personnel and their specialties, evaluation)

Summary

A decision as to the number of languages to be involved in an indigenous author-training workshop should be contingent on the needs of the situation and on recognition of the desired effects. There is merit in both a single language workshop held within the community environs, and a multi-language course held in a more central locale closer to urban areas. Each type has advantages as well as disadvantages.

It is important to plan certain aspects of a workshop well ahead of time, and to ensure that sufficient consultant personnel will be available so that the workshop may be of highest profit to all. Advance information to all participants is of high priority. Sponsoring field linguists should provide as much advance information as possible to the writer-trainees. Consultants should view their roles in the light of their being trained to conduct future workshops where they will, in turn, train others as consultants. Guidelines are briefly outlined to help consultants define their tasks as advisers and encouragers of trainees.

A checklist of logistics has been included to assist the coordinator or director in planning for a smoothly run workshop. While attention to such detail does not spell either success or failure, foresight in the preworkshop phase can make for maximum potential for good outcome.

References

Athey, Irene. Reading research in the affective domain. In Harry Singer and Robert B. Ruddell (Eds.), *Theoretical models and processes of reading.* Newark, Delaware: International Reading Association, 1976.

Crofts, Marjorie. Personal communication. Brasilia, Brazil: Summer Institute of Linguistics, 1978.

Hunter, Georgia. Personal communication. México: Instituto Lingüistico de Verano, 1978.

Murphy, Isabel. What is a writer's workshop? Mimeographed paper. Brasilia, Brazil: Summer Institute of Linguistics, 1977.

Chapter Eight

Trainee in Focus: Classes and Activities

The writer-trainee is the most important figure in the training course. Chapters 8 and 9 focus on workshop content designed especially for the development of the writer, to awaken consciousness as to personal potential as well as responsibility to the community.

No two workshops are alike. Therefore, the reader should understand that activities noted in this section are not intended to be followed slavishly. Rather, the content of this chapter is intended to be helpful for guideline purposes only. Detail has been included in order to give maximum help to those who someday may find themselves in charge of a workshop but without previous experience to rely on (as was the case of this writer in 1970).

Chapter 8 includes the following:

Goals of the Workshop
Opening ceremony
The first day
Excursions and Projects
Writing Assignments
Typing Classes
Classes in Mimeographing or Duplicating
Art Classes
Closing Ceremony

Chapter 9 deals exclusively with topics for trainee discussion.

Goals of the Workshop

The principal goals in training the indigenous writers are fourfold: 1) To awaken trainees' awareness of the worth and importance of written literature in the indigenous languages. 2) To help trainees understand their responsibility toward the home community in providing such literature. 3) To help trainees complete one or more pieces of creative writing (amount determined by length of workshop, capabilities of the writer, etc.). 4) To provide each trainee opportunity to take one or more pieces of original writing through the entire process of copy preparation and duplication.

The schedule for each day should contribute in some way to one or more of these goals. All activities, whether educational or social, should aim toward goal fulfillment.

Opening Ceremony

In many countries it is the custom to open special courses, conferences, and seminars with a program which state and local officials are invited to attend and to give words of support to the enrollees. This custom has been observed in several workshops with good effect. Although the program may be brief, an hour or less, it still provides an opportunity for the larger society to be recognized, to become aware of the nature of the course, and to lend its official support to the undertaking. Such a ceremony does much toward establishing in the trainees' minds the realization that the minority language truly is important in larger circles. The minority group realizes that it need not fear disapproval by the larger society; thus one obstacle may be automatically removed from the pathway to success.

The First Day

A workshop schedule may be as casual and flexible as the situation demands. In general, however, it has been found helpful to begin the program on a fairly structured basis, gradually tapering off to more concentrated work on specific writing and duplicating projects.

The first few days are often the most difficult as the new subject is approached and new ideas are considered. Following is a sample of the procedures many have found useful in the introductory phase.

Introductions

Teaching personnel and trainees are introduced to the entire group. Names are given (unless the practice is culturally unacceptable) and the names of towns or villages where the trainees live. The locations are pointed out on a map, if possible. All are asked to give a brief description of the home area and a sample of their language. A greeting or other short phrase from each language is written on the chalkboard.

Purpose of Workshop

In order to clarify the purpose of the course, it has been found helpful to talk about previous workshops, to show pictures or slides of activities undertaken in the courses, and to present samples of books done by other indigenous authors. Usually the trainees are confused about the purpose of the workshop since the concept of writing in their languages may still be very new to them. In the 1970 workshop it was not until their first material had been typed into a booklet format that the trainees began to comprehend the purpose of their work. Several sponsoring field linguists reported hearing the surprised comment, "So that's what we're doing!" Now, after many such workshops, it is relatively easy to procure tangible examples or photos of what can be expected.

Discussion of Why It Is Highly Desirable to Read and Write in One's Own Language As Well As in the National Language

The discussion may bring up the following points:*

• It is easier to communicate with friends and relatives who are away from home, if the communication can be done in writing.

• Your message can be conveyed more easily in your own language than in a second or third language.

• It is easier to express your deepest feelings in your own language rather than in a language learned later in life.

*I am indebted to colleagues Frances Woods and Mary Morgan who shared with me their experiences in conducting workshops in Nepal and Mexico, respectively.

- Those who are literate in whatever language are always held in respect by the rest of the world, whether or not the language is a shared one.
- It is easier to become literate in a second language when you already read and write your own language.
- Books can carry as deep an emotional impact as oral expression.
- Books are "friends"; they can be counted on to help us in many ways. Dictionaries help us, as do books on travel and farming. Books about known things, like birds, fishing, or our own village stories, help us relax and feel at ease. There are books that make us laugh, books that make us weep. Some poetry can touch us very deeply and make us realize how beautiful is our language. As human beings we have many needs and, like friends, books can help to meet those needs. It is easier for our "friends" to help us if they speak our language.

Discussion of How Books Come into Being

There is another human being behind the book which we hold in our hands. In a sense, that person is *talking* to the reader. I, as a reader, am *listening* to what the author says. Instead of one person's mouth and another person's ears, now paper and pencil are the means of sending a message and another person's eyes are the means of receiving it.

Workshop Classes and Activities Outlined

The general program should be outined for the trainees, and the schedule explained. As in all classes, ample opportunity should be given for questions and comments.

Orientation to Discussion Classes

The contribution of each trainee to the class is a very important one. Each one should think how to help another learn. This can be done by setting an example of an attentive attitude, making insightful comments, asking questions about anything that is not clear. These comments and questions are helpful to the leaders and teachers also, for then they know better how to present the material to the whole class.

It is important for trainees to understand that they should all be present at the beginning of classes so they can participate in everything presented. Otherwise, they will miss something important that will help them do the work of that day.

A Tour of the Facility

The trainees are shown the library or reading area and location of offices of the director and of consultants who, of course, are present in the tour group.

Social

A social or some other casual get together may be planned for the evening hours with all workshop personnel, field linguists, and trainees attending. Singing, slides of one of the areas represented, refreshments—all can contribute greatly to the establishment of an esprit de corps, an important element in such a workshop. Whatever the nature of the recreational time, it is important that all staff, field linguists, and trainees attend and participate, to ensure a feeling of oneness.

Interviews

Early in the workshop, time should be allocated for personal interviews with the trainees by the director or consultants. Data that may indicate special direction for the trainee's program should be recorded (See sample 4 in Appendix B).

Excursions and Projects

Visits or excursions may be made to various points of interest in the region around the town or center where the workshop is held. Usually one or two such visits are made each week during the first part of the workshop. Later, as trainees become more intensively involved in finishing their literary projects, there is little time, need, or even desire for excursions.

Various purposes may be accomplished by these planned trips. The principal one is to expand the trainees' knowledge of the world outside their own spheres, and to give them something new to write about. Whether it will be published is a decision they will make later. Some trainees have learned the skill of note-taking during these visits. The trips also further the spirit of camaraderie among the trainees and teaching personnel which is an important element in a workshop program. Much can be learned about individual trainees during these expeditions: aggressiveness, shyness, humor, sensitivity, depth and area of interests, leadership abilities, concern for others—all come to the surface much more easily in the informal atmosphere these trips generate.

It is highly important, before embarking on an excursion, to discuss with the trainees the significance of the activity they will observe. For example, if they are going to visit a factory, they should know something about the product and its value to society. Perhaps they should become aware of the significance of mass production in order to meet a large demand and hence the need for a factory. Many other aspects may be brought to their attention such as the process itself (which can be very confusing if they are unaware of what to expect), labor, management, and cost accounting.

Examples of excursions include visits to a factory; a weaver's shop; a museum, especially if areas of life as known to the trainees are depicted; a water-purifying plant; a model farm; a city library; a candy or cookie factory; the airport; a printshop; the telegraph office; a radio station; the zoo (usually the most popular of all); and rides on a train or a launch.

Projects have included such things as learning how to use a telephone, how to bake banana bread, how to make compost as garden fertilizer, how to graft fruit trees, and how to raise rabbits. Making a small oven from an empty metal container has been a very popular project.

Learning how to relate, in writing, new experiences in terms meaningful to home audiences should always be the ultimate aim of the activity.

Writing Assignments

Opportunity should be given to the trainees to write on any topic they may feel burning within their souls. Perhaps some have already tried their hands at writing; it is good to recognize and encourage this. Most of all it is important to help the trainees realize at the outset that formal structuring will be kept to a minimum and their creativity in writing is the desired norm. It should be clearly understood that the workshop leaders fully recognize that each language represented has its own style, and that no one proper style of writing is going to be forced on them in the course. This is often a difficult concept to get across at the beginning, and is best done by good consultant technique, i.e., the consultant refuses to be pressured into stating whether something is poorly expressed and how to improve it. Instead, the consultant seeks to develop the trainee's confidence and ingenuity in verbal expression. If other speakers of the language are present, their help may be sought.

As to topic, it often happens at the course's initiation that trainees will have no idea what to write about since they have not been thinking along such lines. Successful stimuli have been found in the form of pictures or photos applicable to the trainees' culture, or by exhibiting artifacts brought from the areas represented. These are displayed and the question asked: What event does this remind you of, either in your life, or in that of a friend or relative? Thus the desired atmosphere is created from the start as trainees share their experiences. In one workshop a trainee was reminded of an amusing canoe mishap. His account brought forth a rash of canoe stories, generating a great deal of hilarity—and several good stories. Most important, an excellent atmosphere for writing was created instantly.

Some trainees may want to draw pictures, and then explain in writing what they have drawn.

Sometimes contrasting cultures, as depicted by pictures from different areas, stimulate ideas for writing. This is not a new notion, of course. It has often been used in writing classes in American schools. In teaching a high school class in creative writing, Burkhart (1974:15) reported her use of simultaneous three-screen display of color slides in which contrasting local homes were flashed before the students' eyes:

> . . . an old Victorian mansion, a Wuthering Heights farm house, a modest, but substantial family dwelling, a ghetto-looking apartment facade . . . the slides invited immediate comment as students entered the classroom. A short story writing unit was launched.

Music was also used at times by Burkhart to stimulate imagination and create the appropriate mood.

Obviously this type of writing is for a phase far advanced over the initial stages of writing in a beginning indigenous writer workshop. Nevertheless, it shows the usefulness of contrast as a pump-priming device, and of the necessity of setting a mood.

Some workshop leaders have found it helpful to begin with a Stage 2 assignment rather than with Stage 1. A favorite topic is the trip to the workshop in the form of a letter home. This brings two important elements into focus: 1) writing to a specific audience and 2) writing from one's own experience.

If the trainees have been educated in the national language, they may be tempted to write first in that language and then translate their work into the local language. Therefore, it should be clearly stated at the beginning of the workshop that all writing must be done first in the indigenous language even though initially it may seem awkward to the writers. Eventually, however, their writing will become clearer, more cultural and vivid if they first think and then write in their own language. Otherwise, in translating from the second language, they will be likely to follow that langugage's thought patterns and idea sequences, and will risk loss of richness and uniqueness of thought patterns and expressions in the mother tongue.

Since the objective of the first few assignments is to get the trainees into the mood of writing with freedom to express themselves clearly, it is advisable to put little or no emphasis on the mechanics of spelling or paragraphing. That can come later at a more advanced stage. If writers have difficulty spelling because they are unfamiliar with the orthography, the sponsoring field linguist should be readily available for help. However, care should be taken not to turn this moment into linguistic research or even a teaching session on orthography unless the trainees strongly desire it.

Too often creativity has been completely stifled as the trainer peers over the budding author's shoulder and points out errors in spelling, punctuation, paragraphing or even in expression of thought. There may come a time for this, but not in the beginning phase. The important activity at this stage is the production of interesting material, a difficult task in itself.

If necessary, writing per se should be abandoned and a tape recorder used in order to ensure the attainment of the underlying objective. Perhaps the author is illiterate, in which case the use of the recorder is imperative. At this point the field linguist becomes a stenographer and considers the job of transcription an important service in order to reach the objective of beginning a written indigenous literature.

Emotive content helps a story come alive to the reader. However, putting emotion into the story is not easy for beginning writers, and they may completely fail to do so in early attempts. Therefore, it is important early on to get the trainees thinking about how to make their stories and narratives so vivid that readers will sense the same emotions and physical feelings the writer experienced.

To stimulate expression of emotion in writing, an assignment may be given to describe a very happy time in life, a very sad time, something "scary," or a physically difficult experience.

The following example, translated into English by its Gude author (Nigeria), represents such an exercise:

> . . . . the rain started to beat us from there up to Panshanu near Jos and it was in the night. We came on the lorry, like on the mountain of the hail, because the cold was too much. The whole blood in our bodies was weak like a drain during the dry season because of the cold. Everyone was shifting to one another to share the warmth from the bodies, but it was unfortunately. The time we had arrived we were unable to eat because there was too much cold and it was raining again.

Ask the group questions such as: Did you also feel the cold the author experienced when riding at night in the back of the truck? What words did he use that made you realize just how cold he felt?

Even relating an experience as recent and vivid as the trip to the workshop does not always free the trainees to the extent that they are able to write really interesting accounts. Frances Woods (1978) lists a number of ideas that are sometimes helpful in getting trainees into the thought patterns most likely to be productive:

> • Think of someone in your village who is especially good at telling stories and communicating happenings around the village. Use that person as a model. How would the person tell it? What words would you expect to hear?

> • Think of your audience. Who will read your book? Your wife? Your husband? Your best friend? Your

mother? Your father? Write for these people, not for yourself. You want them to understand and to enjoy the things you enjoyed and to be sad over the things that made you sad, etc. Remember, don't write for your linguist.

• First of all, think of what you want to say. In your mind, go over the details, and then think about the order in which you want to present these things in writing. Later on, as you go on excursions to various places, look at everything. If you want to, make notes to help you remember what you see and hear. Then write about these things as soon as you can; otherwise you may forget them.

• Look at what you have written and ask yourself these questions: Did I say what I wanted to say? Does the reader need further clarification or explanation? Are there ineffective or useless words or phrases that I should omit?

• Read what you have written to other speakers of your language. How do they react? Do they like it? Understand it? Think it's too long or too short? You may need to make some changes. It may be even more effective if you give your piece of writing to other speakers of your language and ask them to read it for themselves.

• Don't be afraid or ashamed to rewrite. Writing is not easy, and we often need to change what we have written to make it speak more clearly.

For some trainees, especially those with more education or experience in the national language, an explanation of the four stages of graded reading material has stimulated inspiration for writing of Stage 1 material. Apparently, the progression of stages legitimizes the use of legends or other stories of purely local origin which heretofore may have been considered useless for purposes of writing.

Whatever the first production turns out to be, wholehearted recognition, praise, and helpful comments by consultant and sponsoring field linguist are essential to encourage the writer to keep writing.

Typing Classes

The question naturally arises as to the value of teaching the trainees to use a typewriter since typewriters may not be easily procured by a local community. It is true that not every community will be able to procure one, but observation has shown that many remote communities in most of the countries where SIL is working do manage to buy at least one typewriter (usually secondhand) for village use. Furthermore, if funds are made available by development agencies, the supply of one or more typewriters should head the list of items to be donated to a community that is on the road to self-sustained literacy. A belief that typewriters will one day be easily available in most locations has been a deciding factor in making typing classes a part of writer training.

From nearly every country contacted, reports indicate that typing lessons generate in the trainees an incredible degree of interest in writing. Some older trainees, whose many years of hard field labor have made their hands too stiff to hold a pencil or pen for very long, have learned to type in record time. One trainee (in a Guatemala workshop) learned so much in just under three weeks of typing classes, one hour a day, that he was able to type his stories as he composed them. This particular trainee had not been able previously to master the skill of writing with either pencil or pen, probably because he had not had sufficient practice in learning to draw the letters quickly.

Some reports indicate that the typing classes increase reading fluency as well as facilitate writing.

If possible, typewriters should be made available to the trainees so they can utilize whatever spare time they may have in practicing their typing and in writing or copying their articles and stories. This has not always been possible in many of the workshops, since the typewriters were available only during certain hours when they were not being used elsewhere. In any case, it is important that typing be taught as a step toward independence in writing and publishing.

The first typing class may include the following:

• Introduction to the machine's operation, and a demonstration of touch typing with discussion as to why this is preferable to the hunt-and-peck method.

- Learning the first keys, with accuracy as the first objective, speed as the second.
- Explanation of a keyboard wall chart.

In the ensuing classes, as soon as the basic letters are learned and a degree of accuracy is attained, the trainees should begin copying lists of words in their own languages—words which contain letters already learned on the keyboard. Without exception, reports indicate that as soon as this stage is reached, the trainees' interest, accuracy, and speed in typing increase noticeably.

Classes in Mimeographing or Duplicating

The usual learning pattern for many indigenous groups is first observing, then doing. This principle may be easily applied to the use of the silk-screen mimeograph or duplicator by planning many opportunities for the trainees to observe it in action. These observation experiences should begin early in the workshop, even before the trainees have fully grasped the import of producing reading material in their languages.

In at least one workshop, the writer-trainees were introduced to the silk-screen mimeograph on the first day of the course and they immediately began to learn how to use it. By the end of the course, they were experts, handling it more efficiently than the teacher.

Just as trainees are instructed in the care and cleaning of their typewriters, they should learn how to clean the silk screen in order to preserve it. These habits are formed neither easily nor quickly, so it is important that adequate time be allowed for observation, instruction, and practice.

Operation of the duplicator offers opportunity for the trainees to work together in teams of three or four: one places the paper in position for printing, the second makes the impression, the third lifts the screen, and the fourth removes the paper. Often great enjoyment and satisfaction come from this cooperative effort, for it frequently fits the work pattern for community projects.

Art Classes

Art work, in the context of writer-training workshops, usually means that the author illustrates the articles written and designs covers for the booklets produced. It does *not* mean the importation of skilled artists to do the illustrations for the trainees.

In many cases, the pictures done by a Western artist are meaningless or, at best, unsatisfactory to some indigenous people. For example, the Guahibo people of Colombia are not at all happy with a picture of just a fish. They must know which *species* of fish is being depicted. There are precise details which absolutely must be included for proper identification of the fish, while other details may be omitted. Anything less is completely unsatisfactory to them.

In the workshop art classes, care has been taken not to impose Western ideas of perspective, proportion, and placement of figures, all of which may be meaningless to some groups. Instead, the trainees are helped to develop their own artistic talents within the art forms of their culture. Such development may not be easy to accomplish, nor is it easy to find consultants who have both artistic talent and sensitivity in appreciating indigenous art forms.

Jo Machin (SIL artist in Mexico) has taught art classes in several workshops, helping the trainees to develop their abilities to their own satisfaction. As experienced as Machin is, she states that at times it is quite difficult to decide whether the picture which the trainee struggles to produce is representative of a true cultural art form, or if it is merely the work of an unskilled trainee who really has no artistic talent.

In some cases it is obvious that the trainee does have a great deal of natural ability. From Colombia came the report that one young man exhibited extraordinary ability in making accurate, detailed drawings of plants and flowers. A national educator, visiting the workshop, was so impressed as he watched the young man at work that he arranged to have the booklet published in color, with text in both the indigenous language and in Spanish. The botanical names were also included.

A young Panamanian, initially discovered in a writer workshop, has gone on to become not only a national figure in the art world, but an international one as well, representing his country at an international book fair in Italy.

Some societies have developed a highly sophisticated artistic sense and are completely self-confident in their ability.

This assurance seems to be characteristic of many of the Pueblo peoples of the United States. A Tewa teacher informed me that whenever one of her young pupils protests an inability to draw pictures, she says, "Aren't you Tewa? If you have Tewa in you, you can draw!" Thus bolstered, the child usually proves the teacher correct.

In many of the Latin American groups, the questions of perspective and proportion are of secondary importance—if they are important at all. Primary consideration is given to focus; the object, the body part, or the person or animal that is the center of attention in the story is often shown to dominate the scene with respect to size (see Figure 3).

A series of events is often depicted in circular or zigzag formation, rather than by a left-to-right linear sequence (see Figure 4).

One writer used a "layering" effect to depict story sequence (see Figure 5).

It was found that the Cacua people of Colombia immediately recognized the outlined, featureless figures done by a Cacua writer, when the completed booklet was displayed in the

Figure 3. Emphasis on object focused on in the story.

Contrasted with the tiny canoe and its occupant, the tiger is depicted as an enormous animal since it is the subject of the story. In the mind of the illustrator, the human element is incidental to the plot. (Illustration done by Jorge Valencia Rodriguez, a member of the Carapana group of Columbia.)

home community. The field linguist was startled to note that the readers knew not ony *what* the figures represented, but *who* they represented. Repeatedly she heard the Cacua equivalent of, "Hey, look! There's Joe!"

The significance of helping people to utilize their own artistic abilities within their cultural art styles cannot be overemphasized from the standpoint of a continuing program of indigenous literature.

Figure 4. Story sequence in zig-zag formation.

Explanation of story sequence in Figure 4.

1. The rabbit was eating beans.

2. Every day the owner of the beans went to look at the beans.

3. He arrived. The rabbit was there.

4. The owner went to put up a "soldier of beeswax." He arrived and put up the "soldier." And the rabbit arrived. (The rabbit proceeded to try to engage the "soldier" in conversation, kicked him when he didn't answer, and got stuck to him. The owner returned and grabbed the rabbit.)

5. He took him to his house.

6. He put on a pot of hot water.

7. He put the rabbit inside a net bag. The coyote arrived. (The rabbit told the coyote he was waiting to be married to an important woman, and the coyote demanded that the rabbit get out of the bag so he could take his place. The rabbit obliged, and it was the coyote who was scalded by the hot water brought by the owner. The coyote broke out of the bag, found the rabbit and threatened to eat him, but the rabbit pointed out a tasty "sheep's head" to eat instead.)

8. The coyote went over. He took the "sheep's head" in his mouth.

9. And wasps flew out! (Badly stung, the coyote went to accuse the rabbit and then died. The rabbit was happy, declared himself safe, was chased by an eagle, and hid under a maguey, where a snake grabbed and killed him. Another rabbit arrived and said, "You have died. I'll go on wandering. I may die or I may escape.") (Machin, 1981:8)

Figure 5. Layered effect.

Action in this story begins in the lower righthand corner (1), moves up to the next level (2), and is completed on the top level (3), terminating in the upper lefthand corner. (Illustration done by a 14-year old Eastern Popoloca youth of Mexico.)

Trainee Classes and Activities   123

Closing Ceremony

Attendance of interested officials at a closing ceremony may be even more important than their presence at the opening. Without exception, every workshop report noted that the workshop ended with a program to present something of the process of training and the materials which resulted: booklets, newsletters, and even the manuscripts still in process. This display of work never fails to capture the interest of the invited educators and other officials, who now see indisputable proof of the capabilities of the indigenous groups.

As a part of a closing ceremony in Colombia, three trainees gave a demonstration of touch typing. As soon as they finished, the official visitors leaped to their feet and converged upon the three to verify that the material just typed was indeed the same as what the typists had been given to copy, and that no hoax had been played. The demonstration apparently dissolved any hidden doubts the officials may have had concerning indigenous people's ability to enter the modern world of literature and education. The visitors were then able to express warm and enthusiastic appreciation for every aspect of the work accomplished by all the trainees.

In Guatemala, one official visitor (a former university rector) was deeply moved by the presentation of poetry in one of the indigenous languages, as well as by the other writings. Requesting permission to speak extemporaneously, he evaluated the workshop results as a highly significant demonstration that "Mayan literature is not dead as some claim, but very much alive."

Certificates presented by one or more of the visiting officials climax a closing program. For some trainees, possession of a certificate is of highest importance; perhaps it is the only one they have ever received. And to have earned it through the medium of their own language conveys a significance which is difficult for those from the industrialized world to appreciate.

Summary

Goals for training writers must be established as benefitting both the individuals and the communities they represent. Once defined, these goals should guide every activity and writing assignment.

This chapter has taken into consideration both generalized and specific activities reported by SIL colleagues as useful and effective in indigenous writer workshops.

Of highest importance is the incorporation of indigenous cultural style, whether it be in writing, in art forms, or in cooperative effort to produce a piece of literature in its final form. It is also important that formal opportunity be given to representatives of the dominant society to see, understand, and appreciate the capabilities of the indigenous society for operation in this medium.

Together with Chapter 9, this chapter should give helpful guidelines to anyone who wonders just how to go about holding an indigenous writer-training workshop.

References

Burkhart, Dorothea. Writing short stories. In Patricia Geuder, Linda K. Harvey, Dennis Loyd, and Jack D. Wages (Eds.), *They really taught us how to write*. Urbana, Illinois: National Council of Teachers of English, 1974.

Machin, Jo. What about visual esthetics? An open letter to NOL readers, *Notes on Literacy*, 1981, *35*, 1-9.

Morgan, Mary. Personal communication. México: Instituto Lingüístico de Verano, 1978.

Woods, Frances. Personal communication. Dallas, Texas: Summer Institute of Linguistics, 1978.

Chapter Nine

Trainee in Focus: Discussion Topics

Obviously, there can be no single set of instructions as to how or what the trainees are taught in discussion sessions. Each workshop will differ drastically from another according to the level of sophisticaton, experience, interests, and abilities represented in the group. However, the following is a compilation of topics which have been reported as useful by various SIL colleagues involved in writer-training workshops. Many of the topics cited are variations of those discussed by Wendell (1975).

Nearly all those reporting agree that a discussion session is usually superior to a lecture, although there may be exceptions. However, the best learning takes place when the trainees are actively engaged in thinking of and verbalizing the various facets of a particular topic.

The following are the topics most used in the workshops for initial writer training. Each topic is then elaborated by either a description or a listing of salient points in the form of questions to be discussed.

1. Communication within the local community
2. How to classify easy and difficult reading material
3. Selecting your audience
4. Which language to use
5. Taking notes
6. Using the five senses in writing
7. Different types of literature
8. Local history and its relationship to national history

9. Heritage
10. Social change, social stress, and the generation gap
11. Editing
12. Letters
13. Responsibility toward the entire community's literacy problem
14. Calendars
15. Newsletters
16. Format of a booklet
17. Economics of publishing

Communication within the Local Community

Objective: That trainees recognize the efficiency of oral communication procedures in various societies and the advantages and disadvantages of written communication.

Sharing News

In what situations do people share news and information? Is there a regular time set apart for this, e.g., once a week at the market.

What kinds of news or information are shared? Public announcements? Social affairs? Secret news? Teaching of new and old ways?

What is the need for communication within a community? To communicate traditional values and lore to future generations? To exchange useful information within a language or linguistic community? To communicate useful information from the outside world? To erradicate false notions? To warn others of impending dangers?

The following are examples of the means of conveying or announcing messages and information:

Objects
message ropes (with knots tied at intervals) as in the Philippines
message sticks as among the Austalian Aborigines
types of nuts, leaves, and stones, as in Nigeria (to announce that a hunt is to take place)

Nonverbal sounds
drums (Nigeria)

brass gongs (Philippines)
whistle talk (Mexico)
tolling of church bell (Mexico)

Speaking
by radio
gossiping at the well, in the market, on the trail
public announcement by town officials

Writing
letters
newspapers, books, posters

Demonstration or drama

Who are the agents of communication? Village elders? Village seer or shaman? Intermediaries? Announcers? Parents? Children sent by parents? Who else passes on information, news, and traditions within your area?

What are the most important kinds of information? How do you know that it is the most important, i.e., what are the signs that tell you of its importance?

Does everyone in the community hear the message? What happens if someone doesn't hear it? Whose responsibility is it to inform everyone?

Where or what are the centers or places of communication? In people's homes? On fuel gathering expeditions? At the village well? On hunting expeditions or drinking parties? At communal activities, as farming or house building? At the train station? In the public square? In the area in front of the chief's house? At school? At fiestas or parties? At the home of the man who owns a radio or television set? At a religious center (church, temple, mosque, shrine)?

What is the value or advantage of reading and writing when there are already efficient ways of giving and receiving news and announcements? (This part of the discussion is especially important and should not fail to be included during a workshop. Later on when struggling writers find the going difficult, they will need to remember the discussion of why reading and writing are of value and importance for their community.)

Telling Stories

In what situations do people tell stories? While working together in the fields? During ceremonial gatherings? At night as the family gets ready to sleep?

Who can tell stories? Can anyone tell stories or only the older people? Are there professional storytellers? Do both men and women tell stories? Do parents (or grandparents or other relatives) tell stories to the children of a family? Are the same stories told to both boys and girls?

What makes a good storyteller? The use of vivid word pictures? The emotion you feel as you listen? The choice of story as fitting to the audience? The teller's knowledge of the subject material? The teller's knowledge of the audience? Good intonation? Gestures?

Do you learn something from the stories, e.g., how your people think? What they laugh about? How they get what they want? What they think about others? What others think about them?

What advantages are there in putting stories into writing? What disadvantages? Are there certain kinds of stories which should not be put into writing? What kinds of stories should be put into writing?

Do people like to hear new stories or do they prefer only the ones that have been handed down through the generations?

How to Classify Easy and Difficult Reading Material

Objective: That trainees recognize the great usefulness of their own stories in helping new readers perfect their skills, and understand how to determine whether a piece of literature is easy to read.

Mary Morgan (SIL, Mexico) has developed the following steps to present the concept of Stages 1, 2, and 3 (see discussion of stages in Chapter 2). She asks leading questions and follows with related exercises:

What do people do in your village? List these activities on the chalkboard. The list probably will include work, festivals, religious activities, and town projects.

What would you like to write about concerning these activities? List your choices by title.

Are these activities easy or hard to understand? Go over the list and ask if the villagers would understand the setting of your article or story.

Classify the topics in three groups according to difficulty of understanding and reading: 1) easy, 2) a little difficult, 3) difficult.

(Morgan states that such groupings usually follow very closely the classifying elements found in Stages 1 through 3 of the chart. See Figure 1, Chapter 2.)

A simple exercise is given to help the trainees further define the three stages of difficulty in reading as related to the culture.

Suppose that John Doe writes a study of the birds around his home area. Into which group would this writing fall? (Group 1)

If he studies the birds found here in the workshop area, into which group would you put his writing? (Group 2)

Suppose he uses some books to help him do a study of the birds of Europe (or North America or Africa) and he writes an article about his findings. Into which group would the article fall? (Group 3)

Later, when the trainees have authored several articles, Morgan reviews the three stages by means of a similar exercise in which the students classify their own articles according to the above criteria. These are compared for ease of reading with translated materials, introduced now as comprising Group 4.

Selecting Your Audience

Objective: That trainees realize their need to keep specific people in mind as the hearers/readers of their written material.

It often happens that trainees have a difficult time visualizing members of their culture as a reading audience. They are geared to explain certain customs and ways to the field linguist, and view anything that appears in written form as being either for or by the outsider. Therefore, careful check must be made of the first writings, in particular, to make sure that trainees really are addressing appropriate audiences. In the 1970 workshop, one field linguist found that she had to present a verbal picture in order to get a trainee to focus on the audience at home. The trainee was instructed to imagine that she was sitting with the rest of her family around the evening fire, and was asked to name them aloud and to point to the imagined people. This the trainee did, beginning to smile, as she pointed. "Why yes, there is Juan, and there is Pancho, and there is my father, and there is my cousin..." and so on until she had named them all and had visualized them sitting in their customary places beside the fire. She discussed what they were talking about, what they were eating, and what plans they might be making. Then she was asked to choose *one* of the family group to whom she would tell her story. This exercise served well to put her into the mood of addressing the proper audience and focusing on specific people.

New writers tend to generalize their audience. When a trainee in an African workshop was asked specifically for whom he was writing, he said, "For the young people at home who are the members of the church." Such an audience was too nebulous so he was asked to pick out one or two people representing the group and address his work to them, making the subject so clear that these particular individuals would easily understand. His writing then became much more vivid.

Which Language to Use

Objective: That trainees become fully aware of the inherent value of their own language as a vehicle of written communication, in that it has the same qualities as a dominant language except for widespread use.

Classes for the trainees should include focus on the structures of their own languages as distinct from the structures of the national or trade language. Points of discussion should include phonology, grammar and semantics. The objectives for such focus are: 1) To help the trainees see why there are differences in alphabets. 2) To point out that spelling patterns of words differ from language to language; therefore, it is important to practice typing in one's own language to help train correct responses to what the brain tells the fingers to do, and these "orders" will be different for different languages. 3) To point out that there are both similarities and differences in grammatical structure from language to language. 4) To show why word-for-word translation leaves the reader confused.

If the trainees have had only a brief period in school in the national language, they are probably aware of something called grammar, but may not be very clear as to what it means. Usually, classes in the grammar of the trainee's language prove to be very exciting, for this may be the first time they have seen that their language has as much structure as does the national language.

The presentations should encourage trainee participation and should begin with short and simple contrasts. For example, one workshop director begins a discussion of grammatical structure by asking different trainees to write on the board such expressions as *our house, your house, their house.* The possessive morphemes are then pointed out as "structure." A comparison is made with similar structural forms in other languages. It may be pointed out that certain features have a counterpart in the national language and others do not. This is an important teaching for those who have had an overdose of "that which constitutes a *real* language."

Semantic comparisons between languages may be made showing that sometimes there are one-to-one equivalences and sometimes none at all. For instance, in some of the Mayan languages, the way an animal's paw turns, expands or contracts can be stated clearly in one word. However, these words are almost untranslatable into either English or Spanish without at least a short paragraph of explanation.

Contrary to expectations, a clearly presented, inductive study of the phonological and grammatical systems of the trainees' own languages often produces an interest and excitement in the study of language structure that would amaze the average high school English teacher in the United States.

Taking Notes

Objective: That trainees become aware of the value of taking notes as memory joggers and that they learn something of the technique.

An introduction to the subject of taking notes might go something like the following:

> One problem which confronts us all is how to get ideas for new material. We want to continue writing, but what will we write about when we get away from the workshop and the stimulus it gives us?

When we go on our excursions, we see many new things, and we need to take notes so we will not forget the important things. But we can't write down everything immediately, and how do we sort out the important things to note? The following is a list of suggestions of what to do and what to look for.

Use a small notebook that will fit easily into your pocket, and a pencil or a ballpoint pen. Thus you will have something with you at all times to use when an idea comes or when you see or do something that will make for a good writing experience.

First, note very briefly the observed facts. Full sentences are not necessary; instead, write just a few words to help you recall the facts later.

If necessary, and if possible, ask questions about what you do not understand. It has been said that the only stupid question is the one that was not asked.

In addition to the facts observed, note your own reaction or opinion, and those of others. Are you and they laughing, crying, screaming, running, applauding, or standing transfixed?

What is the outcome or end result, if known? Note this in a few words. If it is not known, make note of that.

Is there some generality or lesson that you can draw from this experience or observation? An application that can be made to your life or to others of your community? Something that could be adapted to your way of life? Something for you and your neighbors and friends to avoid? Note these generalities in a few words.

As soon as possible afterwards, sit down and write the experience the best way you can. Later, reread and rewrite.

The above instructions may be used as one facet of preparation for the second or third excursion. Following the excursion, a discussion session may be held to review the note-taking exercise, and to see what problems the trainees encountered in taking notes.

Perhaps the trainees will not need to take any notes, for they may have so trained their faculties of observation that it will not be necessary. However, as new experiences accumulate there may be confusion as to detail and they will need to do something to help them keep the facts straight.

Use of the Five Senses in Writing

Objective: That trainees become aware of their use of the senses, which ones can be described verbally, and whether this usage enhances their writing.

A common device to train American students to write more vividly is to draw attention to the use of the five senses.* The student must find descriptive words that clearly portray sight, sound, smell, taste, and touch as they relate to a particular object. The average high school student is amazed to find how many different ways the English language provides for describing such.

Some leaders of indigenous writer workshops have experimented with exercises designed to bring forth similar responses. One such exercise is to identify and describe objects as they are passed around from hand to hand among the blindfolded trainees. Although the exercise usually produces merriment, it may also produce bewilderment. The trainees usually either identify the object or say they do not know what it is, but give no descriptive terms. Consistent failure to comply makes one suspect that extensive verbalization of this type may violate a cultural norm.

Frances Jackson (1978) experimented with the following exercises in a workshop for bilingual school teachers of the Mississippi Band of Choctaws in an effort to encourage the use of the senses in writing Choctaw. The exercise proved to be so difficult that Jackson decided to abandon the project.

Colors

List as many colors as you can think of in your language.

Under each color, list objects that might be described as having that color.

Choose one or two of these objects and tell why they mean something to you or write a poem or a song about them.

Compare the colors.

What kind of person likes such and such a color?

What scenes or thoughts or ideas are brought to mind as you look at these colors?

How are specific colors used in your culture?

Sounds

Wind: What does it sound like around a house? On a barren hilltop? Through pine trees? Through cracks in a wall or around windows? At different times of the year? At different strengths?

Rain: The same as above.

---

*This topic has been found to be unproductive in many cases. Emotions, especially joy and fear, seem to be much easier for indigenous people to describe than are indications of the five senses. Nevertheless, the topic is included here on the chance that a group may be found that does enjoy talking about one or more of the senses. In such case I strongly invite commentary on the findings with a report of procedure used.

Animals: Domestic, wild. What do they sound like when fearful? When hungry? When angry? When contented?

Walking on different types of ground: wet, icy, snowy, dry, muddy, grassy.

Seasons: Spring, summer, fall, winter, rainy, dry.

Feelings

How do you feel when it's raining? When it's cold? When the wind is blowing? On a hot summer day?

How do you feel when you touch something prickly? Cold and clammy? Muddy? Soft? Furry?

Smells

In the kitchen when your favorite food is being cooked.

Of springtime or other seasons.

Of the woods, a printshop, the schoolroom.

Tastes

Describe your favorite food or dish.

Describe a new food you did or did not like.

Different types of literature

Objective: To increase the trainees' awareness of different types of literature, and to challenge them to think in terms of how these different modes can be expressed in their languages.

Fables and folktales, riddles and proverbs are the obvious and highly useful sources of material for writing and usually prove to be extremely popular. In one workshop, some of the trainees were older and somewhat more sophisticated in background, having traveled to other countries for study in community development, etc. To these trainees, the idea of writing fables excited little apparent interest. They adopted something of a joking, slightly disdainful air, "Oh yes, that's what the country people tell ...."

However, there was even less excitement exhibited over the topics they proposed to write, such as "the need for sanitation in rural communities." Then a chart of the four stages of literature was explained, and they saw a legitimate reason for using such things as folktales, riddles, and proverbs to provide the easy reading material new literates would need to maintain their newly learned skill. Disdain was instantly discarded, and excitement mounted as the sophisticates began recounting fables and collecting riddles. A subsequent book on riddles has now gone into its second printing.

Geography and mapmaking are other forms of literature that can be used and fitted easily into the first three stages of literature. For example, a map of the local village would be a Stage 1 item, a map of the market town a Stage 2 item, and a map of the state a Stage 3 item.

Stories are something that everyone loves, but not everyone can tell a story well. This may prove to be a challenge to the writers and may reveal the "naturals." In helping writers to know how a story differs from other types of literature, the word "conflict" may be used to describe a story. This corresponds with "peak" as described by discourse analysts Robert Longacre and Stephen Levinsohn. A brief description of opening, a build-up of the conflict, a resolution, and a closing provide a skeleton format to conform to, regardless of the style in a particular language. It should be stressed again, however, that "fleshing out of the skeleton" is something that should be allowed to develop naturally through the propagation of written literature.

Biography and autobiography. It may take considerable "priming" by a consultant in order to get sufficient details to make a biography or autobiography interesting. Georgia Hunter, at the 1970 workshop, recalled her efforts to get more from Lucia than, "When I was young, life was really hard. We suffered. That's how it was. It's finished." Gentle but persistent questioning and priming eventually brought forth delightful accounts of caring for sheep, guarding them from coyotes, and the joy of finding good pasture.

Drama. In some societies drama carries extremely high cultural value. One SIL colleague conjectures that in India if school subjects were taught through drama, the level of learning would rise very rapidly. People of India enjoy drama to a high degree, staying up into the early morning hours to see a long play through to its finish. Most Africans have an innate sense of the dramatic and enjoy it to the fullest. From Guatemala, Marilyn Henne (1978) explains how a drama was written in a one-week workshop:

> The budding dramatists first developed a plot in their minds and then explained the action and characters to the actors. The actors were to speak whatever they thought was appropriate for the action. They recorded the practice sessions so that the tape could then be transcribed, revised, and kept for future use. This was an attempt to produce natural dialogue and it worked very well.

After seeing a high school play in a nearby city, a Nigerian writer was inspired to write a short drama, and did so using a well-known fable as the plot. The exercise proved to be an excellent teaching device for focus on audience since, at times, the author lapsed into a summary narrative to relate some of the action. It was pointed out that, as author, he had to provide some means of conveying this information to the audience, either by providing a narrator or by changing the dialogue.

Poetry. To date, the best way to inspire the writing of poetry has been to read poetry to the trainees as an example of what can be done. Through discussion, various facets can be brought out, such as the beauty of words, choices of certain words over other words, arrangement of syntax, importance of rhythm and cadence, repetition of thought in slightly varied form, imagery of words used, and expression of deep emotion.

None of the workshop reports indicates any training other than reading aloud to the trainees poetry which had been written spontaneously in previous workshops, by members of the same language group. Poetry in Totonac and Isthmus Zapotec (Mexico), in Quiche (Guatemala), and Engenni (Nigeria) are the only examples submitted so far, other than original hymns. It is interesting to note that poetry was written in these four languages because the authors became so engrossed, so enthralled with the idea of writing in their languages, that emotion reached a deeper level of expression than had been plumbed before. The writing of the poetry was entirely spontaneous in all cases. The Totonac and Quiche poems were written while the authors were attending workshops, but no assignment for such had been given. The Engenni poems were written after a workshop had ended. The author merely filled a small notebook with thoughts revealing love for the land and for the river that flowed through it, and with thoughts that expressed sorrow over the wars which devastated the people. (See Appendix A for examples of poems.)

Some of the more common *songs, chants, and refrains* found within a society are indeed *so* common they are apt to be ignored as possibilities for written representation. The "remembering-songs" that the old grandmother sings softly to herself as she sits outside her house after the work is done, the lullaby refrain sung to the baby who is fighting sleep, the chants to set up a rhythm for group work, the two-line refrains sung by a group to alleviate the misery of bondage and to set at least the spirit free through its expression of hurt—all of these may escape notice as being possibilities for writing material. However, they may speak far more to the heart of a people than dictionaries and "how-to-do-its" for ecomonic improvement.

Local History and Its Relationship to National History

Objective: That trainees become aware of their role as part of a nation through study of their own history, and its significance in national history.

Robert Wasserstrom of Southern Methodist University, while involved in a community development program in the Tzotzil area of southern Mexico, discovered that a number of the older people of the village of Zinacantan still vividly recalled from their childhood events of battle and plundering that occurred during Mexico's Revolution of 1910. One of the Tzotzil writers trained by Wasserstrom and his team interviewed some of these village elders, and recorded their recollections in writing. From his own understanding of the Mexican Revolution, the local writer then showed how these recalled events fitted into the total picture of the Revolution, and what significance the local battles had in shaping the history of modern Mexico.

Not surprisingly, the revealing historical accounts excited much interest among both older and younger people. Because their parents did not speak Spanish, and because of problems in getting news through to remote areas, the older generation had been isolated from national news during that era. Consequently, they had never understood the scope nor the significance of the local events since even their parents had been only fringe witnesses. All that was known at the time was that strange people were killing each other and that donations of food were being demanded of the Tzotzil people. That the entire nation was involved in a revolution had never come through to their parents nor to them.

The younger generation was interested because they suddenly saw their home area as one that was significantly related to the whole nation. They were duly impressed that people, living and known to them, had been eyewitnesses to the exciting events. History became alive.

The booklets proved popular and began a trend toward an interest in reading and then in further schooling. Gradually, other towns and villages sought the help of the visiting community development team, with the stipulation that reading classes in Tzotzil be included in the program.

Discovering eyewitnesses of historical events may be a difficult undertaking during a multilanguage workshop. However, even a discussion of the subject may prove to be an incentive to someone to do such a study. At a brief workshop held during the 1976 session of the Summer Institute of Linguistics for Native Americans, one of the students was inspired to research the life and work of Wovoka, the Northern Paiute who initiated the Ghost Dance cult (strongly developed later by the Sioux) in an effort to drive the white man from the land. In Mexico, a Tojolabal trainee was inspired to write accounts of local heroes who were also nationally known, after he had visited the humble birthplace of Benito Juarez in Oaxaca. The names of the local heroes were vaguely known by the Tojolabal population, but the facts and significance of their deeds were shrouded in the mystery of another language and another era.

In an effort to help Mexican indigenous trainees further develop a sense of national involvement, Hunter (1978) used some of the following devices:

> Introduced singing of the national anthem once or twice a week with musical accompaniment. The group was encouraged to memorize the verses, one each week.
> Discussed in-depth the life, and work of one of two national heroes. This often stimulated good Stage 3 material.
> Called attention to the Mexican flag through raising and lowering ceremonies and discussions of the symbolism. This led to a study of other national flags, and resulted in several trainees writing on the subject.
> Discussed certain aspects of the constitution as well as its history and significance for all Mexican citizens.
> Visited the Gallery of Mexican History as a climax to the various aspects discussed in class.

Since these topics relate well to Stage 3 literature and may take time for thorough study and consideration, Hunter suggests that they comprise the backbone of an advanced writers' workshop.

Heritage

Objective: That trainees become well aware that they have an ancient heritage of which they can be justly proud.

In some workshops it has been apparent that the trainees needed to become aware of the positive aspects of their heritage. For example, Latin American indigenous groups descend from societies highly developed in the arts, architecture, astronomy, medicine, mathematics, and trade. Most modern indigenous groups, however, are completely unaware of that history, even though there may be pyramids or ruins of other ancient edifices very close to their villages. Usually these buildings are thought to be evidence that some ancient race of "beings" had lived there long ago. There is no thought of a relationship of the "beings" to the present day group, nor is there any sense of heritage based on knowledge of great accomplishment by their forebears.

It has been my privilege to escort several indigenous people through the Museum of Anthropology in Mexico City and to show them something of the significance of the charts and artifacts depicting their origin on this continent. In the course of viewing the exhibits, the visitors usually spy an artifact that looks very familiar. A string of beads made of stone, clay, or bone or a particular instrument for grinding corn may bring the past and present together with a jolt. Interest usually mounts high as they begin to put the pattern together, noting and appreciating the grandeurs developed so many years ago. The comment at the end of the tour is inevitably, "Our ancestors certainly were intelligent!" It is said with an attitude of surprise and wonder that such could really be true.

While discussions, lectures, and field trips (to museums or to ruins of ancient pyramids or temples) may or may not have a direct relationship to writing done in a workshop, it has been noted that a clear realization of personal heritage often does much to establish the self-assurance and sense of worth that is so important in development of the writer. One thing is very clear, that a field trip of this type must be preceded by lucid and vivid explanations of the significance of the area to be viewed, and must be followed by an opportunity for creative expression; otherwise, the experience may be meaningless.

Social Change, Social Stress, and the Generation Gap

Objective: That trainees become aware of the scope of social change, how it has affected their personal lives, and how writing about it can help them and others.

Rapid and imposed changes on indigenous societies are keenly felt in nearly every area of life and, in many cases, are cause for pain. Sometimes the injury occurs because of a lack of understanding and respect between cultures. Sometimes the reason is a lack of understanding of the new ways by the older people of the society, or a failure by the younger people to comprehend the significance of the old ways. The subject is a vast one with many facets to be considered; nevertheless, it should not be ignored merely because it presents difficulties.

Sometimes hurt and rage created by injustices are discovered just beneath the surface. Writing about a particular problem often brings some form of release merely because an opportunity has been given for its verbalization. In one workshop, a trainee introduced every piece of writing with a tirade against the dominant society because it disdained his language. This wrath gradually diminished as the author developed more of the creative abilities within himself and became more preoccupied with what he could do with his language in writing than with the opinion of others about it.

In another workshop, a usually pleasant young man revealed a deep bitterness and rage as he wrote about the medical services in the county seat of his home area. The consultant sensed that there was more to the story than appeared on the page. A gentle probing revealed that the young man's brother had died because of what was considered to be carelessness on the part of the hospital staff, brought about by their indifference toward the indigenous community.

Opportunity for a special writing assignment was made available to the young man. He was to go back to the hospital and request an interview with the director. He was to explain that he had been assigned to write, in his indigenous language, an article concerning medical services for the people of his area, and that he needed the help of the director in order to do this. Dressed in his best clothes and armed with a list of relevant questions, the young man followed the instructions. He went back to the hospital and requested an interview which the director of the hospital willingly granted. The ensuing article gave the author and his readers a clearer understanding of the problems faced by the hospital staff. It also provided an opportunity for critical examination of existing standards to determine whether they were being adhered to in the treatment of the sick. Of even greater importance, it gave the hospital personnel a new respect for the indigene who was becoming involved with news media, and a respect for the indigenous language as the designated vehicle. Thus, a way was opened to begin a natural balancing of the social classes as mutual understanding and respect were generated.

A Nigerian writer was concerned about the generation gap appearing in his own society and elected to write about a specific area of misunderstanding: the differences in marriage customs between the old and the new. The writer hoped to assist younger people in understanding why their parents became upset with new ideas. Also, the writer wanted the older people to see that the younger people were involved in a changing life pattern which extended beyond local or familial control.

The following questions are designed to focus attention on and to stimulate discussion of social change and stress:

How has life in your community changed in the past few years?

Do the people of your generation think, act, dress, or work differently from the way your father or grandfather did? How have things changed? Think of various areas of life: work, play, food, crops, travel, language, courting and marriage, death and burial, schooling, religion, and naming of children.

Are all sectors of the society happy with these changes? What are the points of conflict?

Do any of these conflicts arise because of a lack of understanding of how times have changed? What information do people need to ensure better relationships between conflicting groups?

How are conflicts resolved in daily life? Is there a third party who steps in and talks first to one side and then to the other, and then helps both sides to understand opposing points of view?

How can books or pamphlets be of help on a more impersonal level and on a wider scale?

Editing

Objective: That trainees become aware of possible reasons for changing a piece of writing, and how it can be done for best effect.

What is an editor? What does an editor do? Why do all publishing companies, magazines, and newspapers have editors? An editor's job is to answer the following questions:

- Is the content of material submitted for publication right for the magazine/book/newsletter? That is, will the intended audience of the publication be interested in the subject and the way it is treated?
- Does the article speak clearly so the intended audience will want to read it and will understand it?

Since there may not be anyone else available to edit the work trainees have written, the trainees may have to learn how to be their own editors. How can they do this? The following suggestions have proved helpful in several workshops:

Allow the manuscript to rest for a period of from one day to a week, or record the story on tape and then let it rest for a period.

Visualize a specific audience, one person whom you know.

Imagine as completely and vividly as you can that you are that person. Think of his/her background and what she/he does or does not know about the subject you are treating.

Reread (or listen to) the article or story from that reader's point of view. Can you "see" the action, "hear" what went on, "feel" the experience?

Does the language flow smoothly? Are there places that now sound awkward? What would you change?

Do you want to put in more detail? Another episode? Do you want to omit something?

Are there words the reader may not understand? Terminology or words in the national language or concepts known in another culture that may be foreign to the reader?

Are any words omitted that should be in the manuscript?

Have you included sufficient detail? Have you put in too much detail? Are all the details relevant to the subject?

Are the words spelled correctly so that the reader will have no trouble knowing what they are?

Is the paragraphing well indicated? Will the pages look easy to new readers?

An editing session conducted by a Tzeltal (Mexico) instructor who was a writer is reported by Morgan (1978):

> . . . carbon copies were given out of each man's work. The group read each article and discussed it with reference to meaning rather than to style. Tiburcio (the editor) . . . asked the author to explain to him some of the idiomatic expressions which were unfamiliar to him (because he speaks a different dialect of Tzeltal). When Tiburcio was satisfied that the expression was indeed understandable in the particular village where the author lived, he continued reading. When he did not understand what was meant in a passage, he paraphrased it and asked if his interpretation was correct. Sometimes the author wrote a little more in order to clarify a particular passage.

Letters

Objective: That trainees become aware that there are many purposes for writing letters, that language and style differ according to the kind of letter being written, and that certain conventions prescribed by the national postal system must be observed in order to ensure service.

In both Latin American and African workshops that I have directed, a discussion of letters and their purpose revealed that in many preliterate societies letters are viewed as being bearers of only emergency news. When a person receives a letter, therefore, fear immediately strikes the heart for there are only two messages it can possibly bring: severe illness or death of a family member, or a request for funds to help a relative who has fallen into dire circumstances.

In one Latin American country, a young man who had recently learned to write and who wished to write a letter home, concocted extravagant news to include in that letter: he had gotten married and had also found an extremely high paying job. It so happened that neither item was true. However, somewhere in his background the young man had gotten the idea that only matters of extreme importance merited inclusion in a letter. Therefore, he had a problem: In order to write the letter, he had to have important news, so his necessity became the mother of his news invention.

A session on letter writing with the trainees may include the following:

>*Various purposes.* Family news, business, official communicaton, petitions, opinions (e.g., to an editor of a newspaper), protests.

>*Form.* Varies according to purpose.

>*Style.* Varies according to purpose.

>*Language choice.* Varies according to purpose and intended recipient(s).

>*Addressing an envelope.* What goes into the address, its placement on the envelope, placement of the stamp and return address.

>*How the letter is delivered.* How the letter is handled at a post office, how carried to succeeding post offices, finally getting into the hands of the addressee.

>*Assignment.* Write a letter to someone at home, telling about the workshop and send it by mail if postal service is available in the recipient's area.

Experience has shown that attention to letter form as well as content can carry much more significance than might be expected. In one workshop special attention was given to letter writing and the accepted norm of addressing the envelope. Great appreciation was expressed by the trainees, for although they had had some schooling, this was the first time they had received specific instruction concerning proper form. They no longer felt awkward in doing something that the educated world takes for granted.

Practice should be given in the workshop in the writing of at least two kinds of letters with the normally accepted way of addressing the envelope. Even the matter of what return address to use, temporary or permanent, may cause confusion. For instance, a young man with the equivalent of a high school diploma did not really understand the function of the return address on an envelope. In traveling about the country, he consistently used on his letters the local address where he happened to be staying for a few days, and then was perplexed when desired replies did not reach him. He had not used his permanent address, since he believed the local post office would not accept his letter for mailing if it did not have a local return address.

Responsibility toward the Whole Community's Literacy Problem

Objective: That trainees become aware of their responsibility as writers to help others in the community become literate and to expand the production of reading material.

Attention should be focused on the need for total community involvement in a literacy/literature program. Trainees must recognize that they share in the responsibility to keep up the momentum (hopefully already generated) by considering the following:

Why they should continue to write when there is no one giving an assignment and they are completely on their own.

How to keep literature before other members of the community whether they are literate or not.

How to train others who may want to learn to write.

How to find ways of involving the whole community in reading and writing.

How to find ways of funding the production of materials within the society.

One of the dangers of training only one or two writers in a community is the sense of superiority which they may develop and which they may be unwilling to relinquish to other potential writers. This problem was noticeable among the Munduruku of Brazil. The self-image of the new author-typist-printer was so elevated that he assumed he could do anything he wished, even to using another person's property (such as a bicycle) without asking permission. He further assumed that he had nothing more to learn and during a second workshop was not happy about the suggestions offered for improvement of his work. One incident, however, served well to show him that he had not yet "arrived." In duplicating the cover for his booklet, he erred in planning and ran the coverstock backwards, so that the title came out on the back of the book instead of the front. This incident did much to normalize his concept of his own abilities, and to make him a more sympathetic trainer of others.

Another problem arose among the Munduruku because a woman trainee who had shown much promise in developing creative ability in writing was effectively removed from the literature/literacy scene by her nonliterate husband. Instead of becoming a contributor to the training program as she was well able to do, she was relegated to work in the forest collecting rubber. A cultural norm had been violated; her husband felt threatened and he had to do something to regain control of his position. The reporting field linguist felt this problem could have been avoided if, in the beginning, the linguistic team had sought to also involve the husband in learning to write or in a related activity. Instead, they had focused on a search for talent and quick productivity. They found the talent, but lost all productivity because of a failure to pay attention to social and personal relationships, and to the goal of involving as many people as possible in a writing program.

It must be remembered that many different talents are needed in the production of literature, such as:

> Idea men, the visionaries who can look ahead and envision possible goals and means for attaining them.
> Planners, who can determine the steps needed to arrive at goals.
> Writers, who can put the ideas into action and onto paper.
> Editors, who check details of grammar, punctuation, clarity, and readability.
> News-gatherers, typists, printers, and organizers of distribution channels.
> Treasurers, who know how to keep careful accounts, to warn others of impending financial disaster, and to assist in wise expenditure of funds.

Calendars

Objective: That trainees think of ways to relate the calendric system of the larger society to their own calendric system and how to depict the relationship.

Group discussion may focus on the use of calendars as a way of helping the society orient itself to the time system of the larger, national society, or of representing its own calendric system as an alternative. For example, calendars reflecting the society's work cycle often prove very interesting.

For many years the Mazatec people of Mexico have been very proud of calendars which incorporate both the Gregorian and Mazatec calendric systems. The names of the Mazatec months are noted in the Gregorian numbered square, marking the beginning day of the Mazatec month. These calendars have been tremendously popular, principally because the Mazatecs are able to show others that they also have a calendar.

A calendar for the Guahibo people (Colombia) indicates the seasons when certain wild fruits are found in the jungle. In a similar effort the Yucuna (Colombia) artist-writer trainees drew pictures to represent the seasons when different foods become available. The pictures were arranged in a circular pattern on a posterboard with a Gregorian calendar pad fastened near the bottom.

Many African societies have the system of naming days according to the local town or village which schedules market for that particular day. Calendars reflecting this market location system have been published in different localities.

The making of twelve one-month calendars reflecting either both systems or just the indigenous system can be a very worthwhile project to stimulate group involvement in a writing/printing/distribution project. The current month's calendar on one side with brief news items on the other side has stimulated interest in reading in some areas. People look forward to buying each successive monthly calendar.

Newsletters

Objective: That trainees become aware of the usefulness and comparative speed of production of short newsletters as a way of incorporating reading and writing into the life of a community.

In view of the difficulty which may be found in publishing pamphlets and booklets on the local scene, the easiest place to begin may be in the form of a newletter. There are many advantages including ease of involving a number of people with varying skills, simplicity of format, minimal price, and brief articles on a variety of topics, thus hitting a wide range of interest.

Several indigenous groups are acquiring small silkscreen mimeographs and are experimenting with newsletter production as a means of bringing reading material regularly before the public. These efforts are the results of projects in which workshop trainees have cooperated to produce a newsletter in which one of their articles has appeared. Putting a newsletter together calls for a group organization to decide who should be involved with format, typing, paste up, stencil cutting, duplicating, collating, and distribution.

The following discussion guide is adapted from Wendell (1975).

VILLAGE NEWSLETTER (Discussion Guide)

a. Discuss the need for abundance of reading material. A newspaper is a meaningful way of increasing the amount of reading material.

b. What newspapers are published in your area? Where? What are their titles? Why do you think those titles were chosen? What messages do they convey?

c. Value of a small, one-sheet newspaper:
> inexpensive
> encouraging to new literates or semiliterates—
>> provides small chunks of reading material
> can be produced quite fast
> keeps reading constantly before the public, with
>> minimal effort
> can start small and grow

d. Content—what sections do you like to read in a newspaper? (List)

e. What kinds of news should go into a village newsletter—local, national, or worldwide?

f. Local types—what content?

Does the Chief ever have something he wants to say to everybody?

Would he like to do it by this means?

Do prices fluctuate on local crops? Would this be helpful information for the people? Why?

Dates of fiestas or holidays, market days in conjunction with the Gregorian calendar (these could occupy one side of the sheet)?

Arrivals, departures—young people going away to school, returning from school for holidays?

Names of new school teachers?

News in connection with local churches—special meetings, projects (past and future)?

Trip to another town?

A proverb, verse of Scripture, or short fable?

Obituaries?

If sports groups exist, news of their games, players, schedules?

New seeds available for sale? Where?

Literacy classes?

Medicines for people, animals?

Official announcements (local, state, national)?

g. How many items would you put in one issue?

h. Size of newsletter—letter, legal, doublespaced, two columns?

i. How many copies would you run the first time (better to run out, than to have a lot left—maybe 20-25)? Give one to the Chief and other important people?

j. Employ sellers—let them make a profit?

k. Make sure your facts are accurate. If you quote prices or dates, make sure they are typed correctly.

l. Get other people involved as soon as possible—reporters, typists, duplicator operators, artists, cartoonists?

m. How often should the newsletter be published? Weekly? Monthly?

n. Invite letters from readers—how?

Format of a Booklet

Objective: That trainees become aware of the necessity of and reasons for conformity to certain conventions in planning a booklet, and how to prepare a dummy booklet before typing the stencils.

Discovering the intricacies of making a booklet was a revelation and a great satisfaction to the previously cited Nigerian writer-trainee who, at the end of a workshop, told me how his mental picture of printing had changed. He now understood that feeding a lot of paper into "the engine" from one side did not mean that a neatly bound book would promptly emerge from the other.

Like his companions in the workshop, the trainee had struggled to learn to write interesting material, to type, to select material for a booklet, and to produce that booklet in finished form. He had discovered that it took a great deal of careful and detailed planning and work before the duplicating process could actually begin. He had learned that certain steps must be followed conscientiously if an attractive booklet is to result, with its pages in the right order and its printing right-side-up. Thus, he had concluded that producing a booklet was not the automatic and mysterious process he had once considered it to be.

Workshop instructors have also struggled with the process, not always sure that they, themselves, knew just what to do in order to produce a booklet of more than two pages. It was even more hazardous as they attempted to explain the steps to the trainees.

It is hoped that the steps* shown in the following pages will prove helpful to other instructors and eventually to other trainees who may be going through the same struggles. Five major areas will be covered:

1. Basic decisions to be made before typing
2. Typing the material
3. Preparing a model or dummy
4. Preparing and running the stencils
5. Making the cover

*Based upon suggestions of Frances Jackson (Colombia), Robert Koops (Nigeria) and Isabel Murphy (Brazil).

1. *Basic decisions to be made before typing*
     Dimensions of the book, e.g. pocket size or larger (one-half of legal size paper).
     Diglot or monoglot? (Monoglot: Text in indigenous language only. Diglot: Text in both indigenous language and national/trade language.) If diglot, where will the translation be placed? Alongside the original text, at the bottom of the page, or in the back of the book? Should there be a complete translation or a summary only? What size type should be used for the translation?
     If there is an introduction, what do you want to say? What should be included that will make it easier for anyone who picks up this book to determine what it is all about? Should there be something concerning the orthography so readers will know what the symbols stand for?
     What chapters or story headings will you want?
     What will be the title? A title should be fairly short but give the gist of your article.
     What kind of illustrations? What is their purpose? Where should they be placed in relation to the story? Should they mark the beginning of the story, come somewhere in the main body or at the end? Should all of these positions be marked by pictures? If so, should they all be the same size?

2. *Typing the material*
     Prepare a paper guide according to the measurement of the page: A single sheet with a heavy black line outlining the margins.
     Type each page on a separate sheet of paper using the guide beneath the sheet of paper being typed, so you won't go outside the margins.
     Type the story or article leaving space where desired for pictures, usually at least one-half page, doublespace between lines. Type page number on each sheet in order, with the page number in the same place on each sheet.
     Type the Title Page—title of book, author, language, publisher, date (year), number of copies.
     Type the Introduction.
     Type the Table of Contents, if any.
     If pictures will appear separately from the text, prepare these pages now.

```
+-------------------------------------------+
|                  TITLE                    |
|                                           |
|                 Author                    |
|                                           |
|                Language                   |
|                                           |
|                                           |
|                Publisher                  |
|                                           |
| Date                          No. of copies |
+-------------------------------------------+
```

Read the story through to make sure you have not skipped any lines, and that the typing is correct. This is called proofreading and is a *very important* step.

3. *Preparing the dummy or model*

It may be helpful at this point to show the trainees a printed booklet with staples or stitching removed. Let them look through the booklet first to see how all the pages are numbered consecutively, then spread the book flat and instruct the trainees to lift off the sheets of paper. They should be able to see which page numbers go together, and they will note that very few pages are in consecutive numbering. The following steps will show them how to figure out which pages to put together on one sheet.

Put all the prepared pages in the numerical order in which they will appear in the book. Be sure to include the picture pages.

Count these pages. Divide the total number of pages by four to determine the number of sheets of paper you will need for one book. (Each sheet will have four pages: two on one side and two on the other.) For example, if the book has a total of sixteen pages you will need four sheets of paper. If it has twenty pages, you will need five sheets of paper. If it has twenty-one, twenty-two, or twenty-three pages, you will need six sheets of paper, and some pages will be blank.

Put these sheets of paper together and fold in half.

fold

The folded sheets of paper represent your booklet. *Keeping them folded*, mark each page as follows: On the top page, *in pencil*, write Title Page; on the back of the Title Page write Introduction; on the next page write Table of Contents, if needed. (In some countries, the Table of Contents is placed in the back of the book.) Don't put another page on the back of the Table of Contents unless you have a picture to introduce the first story. On the next page write Page 1. This should be on the right. (Odd numbered pages always appear on the right.) On the back of Page 1 write Page 2. Do the same on each succeeding page, numbering consecutively until you have numbered all the pages of the book. The last page should come on the last of the folded sheets of paper. Now the model (dummy) is ready to use.

Keeping the folded sheets together, paste the typed sheets of the story into the model, making sure the typed page numbers agree with the numbers you have written in pencil in the model.

Now open the model out flat and one by one lift up the large, pasted sheets of paper and look at the numbering of the pages. You will see which pages must go together on one sheet of paper so they will come in the right order when the book is printed, sheet by sheet, on the duplicator.

Now you are ready for the next step.

4. *Preparing and running the stencils*

Type the stencils, sheet by sheet, using your model. Leave the stencil whole if you have a wide carriage typewriter; cut the stencil in half if you have a narrow carriage typewriter. (Measure carefully to determine the place on the stencil which marks one-half of the sheet to be printed.) Odd numbered pages will always be on the bottom half (righthand side) of the stencil, even numbered on the top half (lefthand side). Proofread your stencil and make necessary corrections. This will be your *last opportunity* to remove errors.

Place the pictures just beneath the stencil so they can be traced easily with a soft lead pencil. Be careful not to cut into the stencil.

Using the special backing sheet, draw the traced pictures on the stencil with a stylus or dry ballpoint pen.

Join the cut stencils following the model. Check carefully to make sure you have the pages that go together according to the model.

Run the stencils on the duplicating machine. If the humidity is high, it may be necessary to allow the sheets that have been printed on one side to dry for twenty-four hours before printing on the other side, to prevent the ink from smearing. Check the model to determine which pages go back-to-back.

Run the other side of the sheets, making sure that one side is not upside down. Put each stack of paper together neatly, making sure that all the printing runs the same way.

Collate the sheets following the model. Fold the first booklet exactly in half and check again to make sure the pages are in consecutive order.

5. *Making the cover*

Decide on the color of paper and design to be used.

Prepare the stencil with title, name of author, design (if any).

Run on the duplicator, let dry, fold.

Place the covers on the books and fasten either by stapler or needle and thread. By stapler: The ends of the staples should be on the fold on the inside of the book. Two staples are usually enough. Stapling is generally satisfactory for use in a dry climate. By sewing: Holes may be punched by using a thin nail. Punch five holes, making sure they are evenly spaced. Double sew, using coarse thread or light string.

Your book is now ready to be priced and then marketed.

The Economics of Publishing

Objective: That trainees become aware of the cost of printing and publishing, how to recoup money expended, and how to think of ways of handling the printing projects without depending on outside resources.

Figuring the Cost of Each Book

Keep a record of all the expenses involved in each book, perhaps in a small notebook or on a sheet of paper kept in a safe place where you will not lose it. Example (to be adapted to the local situation):

Expenses for the booklet, *A Canoe Accident*

Paper	$2.00
Cover stock	1.00
Stencils	4.00
Ink	.50
Staples	.20
5 percent cost of duplicator	.30
TOTAL EXPENSE	$8.00

(based on initial cost of $6, to be recouped over a period of time from the sale of several editions)

Cost of each booklet is determined by dividing the total expense by the number of books printed. For example:

$$\$8.00 \div 25 = \$.32 \text{ each book}$$

The *price* of each book will be determined by local mark-up practice, by the demand for the book by buyers, and by any other factors pertinent to the local situation.

Selling

Display your wares. Nobody is going to buy something that is not visible.

Read a little of the most exciting part to your potential buyers so they will know what it is about and how interesting it will be to read.

If someone sells books for you, make sure that the person reads well or can sell effectively without reading. Allow the person to make a profit by selling. If your books are sold in a local store, make sure they are well displayed. Perhaps you need to help the storekeeper by building a bookrack or display case so buyers can see the books easily.

Funding

How does the local community usually raise funds for local projects? The Vagla (Ghana) young people earned money for their literacy projects by hiring themselves out in large groups to do farm work. This project followed their usual procedure for earning money to buy other things used by their group, such as drums for their dances (Herbert, 1979:13).

Discuss with other members of the project committee the details of a revolving fund, such as how much profit should be expected and who will authorize expenditures.

Determine how much should be put aside to be used in purchasing materials for the next publication. Make sure this money is put aside in a safe place.

Summary

The seventeen discussion topics presented in this chapter have ranged from the subjective and philosophical considera- tion of what it means to turn local forms of communication into written forms, to the highly objective, step-by-step proce- dure of preparing a booklet for printing and figuring its cost.

It is not anticipated that discussion sessions will be limited to the topics just presented. The imagination and ingenuity of a workshop director, based upon observation of needs, will stimulate new and beautiful ideas. One criterion must always be kept in view, however—that the new ideas will produce *indigenous* writers and readers who will be able to become independent quickly. Anything that promotes de- pendence upon the foreigner will be self-defeating.

References

Henne, Marilyn. Personal communication. Guatemala: Instituto Lingüístico de Verano, 1978.

Herbert, Pat. Utilising existing social structures for literacy programmes. *Notes on Literacy*, 1979, *27*, 10-13.

Hunter, Georgia. Personal communication. México: Instituto Lingüístico de Verano, 1978.

Jackson, Frances L. Personal communication. Bogotá, Colombia: Instituto Lingüístico de Verano, 1978.

Longacre, Robert, and Levinsohn, Stephen. Field analysis of discourse. Un- published manuscript, n.d.

Morgan, Mary. Personal communication. México: Instituto Lingüístico de Verano, 1978.

Wasserstrom, Robert. *En sus própias palabras.* Mexico: D.F.: Centro Antro- pológico de Documentación para América Latina. Instituto de As- esoria Antropologico para la Region Maya, 1978.

Wendell, Margaret M. Writer-training workshops. *Notes on Literacy*, 1975, *18*, 9-32. (Reprinted in *Notes on Literacy, Selected Articles*, 1979, 251-267.)

Chapter Ten

Field Linguist in Focus: Discussion Topics

If the field linguists attending the workshop have not had previous exposure to or training in literacy programing, it has been found helpful to present separate seminars for their benefit.

Suggested topics for discussion in the field linguists' seminar are as follows:

1. Update on national view of language planning and education of the minority language groups
2. Total literacy program
3. How an anthropological study served as a model for a writers' workshop
4. Theory of "affect" and its relevance to literacy programs
5. The four stages of literature as a basis for determining how to grade reading material
6. Culture change and literacy
7. Development of a written style
8. The reading process: How it is acquired
9. Language awareness as a factor in prereading
10. Testing the reading materials prepared
11. Funding and distribution of materials
12. Continuing indigenous literacy program: Pipe dream or possibility?

These topics will not be discussed at length on these pages. Suggested readings, a central point for discussion, and features for consideration will give guidelines to a workshop leader.

Update on National View of Language Planning and Education of the Minority Language Groups

Reading Fishman, Joshua A. Language planning and language planning research. In Joshua A. Fishman (Ed.), *Advances in langauge planning.* The Hague: Mouton, 1974.

Heath, Shirley Brice. *Telling tongues.* New York: Teachers College Press, Columbia University, 1972.

Central point for discussion

An understanding of the nation's language planning development from an historical point of view, and consideration of current trends especially with regard to education of the linguistic minority groups.

Questions to consider

- What is the national view of language? How did this view arise historically and legislatively?
- How has this viewpoint affected education of the minority groups?
- What budgeting allotment is made for adult education in general? For rural education? For indigenous groups?
- Does the current national policy match current world philosophy concerning indigenous groups as to language and education?
- Is this an appropriate time to expect national approval and support of indigenous literature? If so, how can such support be procured? If not, how can indigenous literature production become self-supporting?

Total Literacy Program

Reading Gudschinsky, Sarah C. Chapter 1, A look at the whole job. *A manual of literacy for preliterate peoples.* Ukarumpa, Papua New Guinea: Summer Institute of Linguistics, 1973.

Gudschinsky, Sarah C. SIL: Literacy policy and its practical outworking. *Notes on Literacy*, 1974, *17*, 22-28.

Central point for discussion
How the Gudschinsky program model may be applied to each indigenous society represented in the workshop.

Questions to consider
- What materials have been prepared or should be prepared in order to take care of the various phases of a literacy program according to the Gudschinsky model?
- How can indigenous literature contribute to each phase?
- How can the various phases be coordinated with phases of linguistic investigation?

How an Anthropological Study Served as a Model for a Writers' Workshop

Reading Worth, Sol, and Adair, John. Navajo filmmakers. *American Anthropologist,* February 1970, *72,* 9-34.
Worth, Sol, and Adair, John. *Through Navajo eyes.* Bloomington: Indiana University Press, 1972.

Central point for discussion
How the experience of training Navajos to make movies can serve as a model for training indigenous authors.

Questions to consider
- What was the purpose of the filmmaking project, and how does it compare with the purpose of a writer-training workshop?
- Compare the two viewpoints concerning the use of films in the study of indigenous cultures

  Indigenous persons are asked to view a finished film and comment on the correctness of its interpretation. (Method commonly used by anthropologists.)

  Teach indigenous persons to use a camera and to do their own editing of the material gathered. (Method used by Worth and Adair.)

How can these approaches to filmmaking be compared to approaches to the literacy problem in preliterate societies?

- Filming involves a three-part consideration: the filmmaker, the film itself, and the viewer. How does this process parallel the production of literature?
- How do details of teaching filmmaking compare with details of training indigenous authors? Consider the following:

> Selection of trainees
> Emphasis: "This is *your* film."
> Instruction given concerning the process
> Teachers easily available for help
> Work organized by trainees
> Quick feedback
> Handling of unexpected reactions and responses of trainees
> Evaluation done by the trainees versus evaluation by the trainers
> Sampling of audience reaction and notation thereof
> Comparison of audience reaction with type of material viewed
> Comparison of anthropologists' ways of teaching with Navajos' ways of teaching

Theory of Affect and Its Relevance to Literacy Programs

Reading   Mathewson, Grover C. The acceptance model: A model of attitude influence in reading comprehension. In Harry Singer and Robert B. Ruddell (Eds.), *Theoretical models and processes of reading*. Newark, Delaware: International Reading Association, 1976.

Central point for discussion
How the application of Mathewson's affective model in a writer-training workshop can have lasting effect on a literacy program.

Questions to consider
- Mathewson says that attitude is a state of readiness for motive arousal. How can this statement apply to

the process of training indigenous authors? How can it apply to Unesco's program of "functional literacy"?

- Trace the exposure to reading by the society with which you are working through the five steps of the affective model: attitude, motivation, attention, comprehension, acceptance.
- Mathewson lists several reasons for motivation including curiosity, exploration, pleasure, self-actualization, achievement, anxiety. Which of these characterize the motivating experience for reading which the society in question has had in the past?
- Mathewson considers curiosity, exploration, self-actualization and achievement to be high on the list of motivating factors. Why does he say that once the first three are built into the reading experience "the achievement motive could wither away ... because the other motives would continue to sustain reading" (p. 667)?
- Why is anxiety the least desirable motive for reading? Has this factor already been built into the societies under present consideration and what is its effect? How can anxiety be alleviated, if not eliminated?
- How can the primary motivating factors be implemented and utilized in a writer-training workshop?

The Four Stages of Literature as a Basis for Determining How to Grade Reading Material

Reading (choose two)

Gudschinsky, Sarah C. Chapter 2, Literature. *A manual of literacy for preliterate peoples.* Ukarumpa, Papua New Guinea: Summer Institute of Linguistics, 1973.

Herzog, Dorothy. A literature workshop: Part I. *Notes on Literacy*, 1974, *17*, 1-6.

Jacobs, Suzanne. Vernacular writing for Micronesians. *Notes on Literacy*, 1977, *22*, 1-18.

Wendell, Margaret M. An experimental project for production of reading material in a preliterate society. *Notes on Literacy*, 1975, *18*, 1-9.

Central point for discussion
　　How the material produced by the trainees in this workshop can be used as graded reading material in literacy programs in the societies represented.

Questions to consider
- List the topics being written about by the trainees. How can these be classified according to Stages 1, 2, or 3? Is there overlap of stages in any of the articles or stories?
- What sampling of audience reaction has been possible during the workshop? With what results?
- What details should be considered for a plan to test the material being produced to determine whether it provides needed graded reading material?

Culture Change and Literacy
Reading (Turner and one other)

　　Achebe, Albert Chinua. *Things fall apart.* Greenwich, Connecticut: Fawcett, 1959.

　　Bowen, Elenore Smith. *Return to laughter.* Garden City, New York: Doubleday, in cooperation with the American Museum of Natural History, 1964.

　　Goodenough, Ward Hunt. Chapter 14. Problems of practice. *Cooperation in change.* New York: Russell Sage Foundation, 1963.

　　Olson, Bruce. *For this cross I'll kill you.* Carol Stream, Illinois: Creation House, 1963.

　　Turner, Charles V. Culture change and the Sina-Sina church. *Practical Anthropology*, 1966, *13*, 103-106.

Central point for discussion
　　How indigenous writers and a literacy program can ease the burden and bewilderment suffered by a preliterate society undergoing change because of contact with a dominant society.

Questions to consider
- With regard to Turner's chart depicting societal reaction to impingement by a dominant culture, how

do the African societies described by Achebe and Bowen, and the South American society described by Olson fit into the rise-fall adjustment pattern indicated on the chart?
- How do the societies represented at the workshop fit into Turner's chart?
- How could indigenous literature and a literacy program assist the African and South American societies in their adjustment periods? How can they assist the society in which you work?

Development of a Written Style

Reading   Duff, Martha. Contrastive features of written and oral texts in Amuesha. *Notes on Translation,* 1973, *50*, 2-13.

Nida, Eugene. Linguistic dimensions of literacy and literature. In Floyd Shacklock (Ed.), *World literacy manual.* New York: Committee on World *Literacy and Christian Literature, 1967.*

Central point for discussion

The gradual and natural development of a written style in a minority language is essential before extensive translation is undertaken.

Questions to consider
- How does Duff classify the changes made by an Amuesha writer in preparing an oral text for publication? Can you surmise the steps in personal development in writing which he had to go through in preparation for such a task?
- What are the advantages of training several productive indigenous writers before engaging in extensive translation work?
- What evidence have you found of the development of an "elegant" writing style in the language you are studying?
- How much reading and writing must be experienced by a society before their writing arrives at points described by Nida as "universals"?

The Reading Process: How It Is Acquired

Reading   Gough, Phillip B. One second of reading. In Harry
         Singer and Robert B. Ruddell (Eds.), *Theoretical
         models and processes of reading.* Newark,
         Delaware: International Reading Association,
         1976.

         Lee, Ernest W. *Literacy primers: The Gudschinsky
         method.* Prepublication Draft, June 1979.
         Dallas: Summer Institute of Linguistics.

Central point for discussion
    To discover the mental processes involved in extracting
    meaning from the printed page.

Questions to consider
- Compare the Gough and Lee models of reading. In
  what areas do they agree? Where do they differ?
- Where does the Mathewson affective model of reading
  overlap with Lee's model of reading?
- What reading experiences do the people of your society
  need in order to attain the fluency these models indicate is the norm? How will these experiences be made
  possible without violating cultural norms?

Language Awareness as a Factor in Prereading

Reading   Barnwell, Katharine. Towards preparing a pre-
         primer. Appendix. Part 2 of *A workshop guide
         for primer construction.* Jos, Nigeria: Nigeria
         Bible Translation Trust, 1979.

         Hunter, Georgia. Chinantec awareness tapes.
         Nova Lit, 1977, *5,* 12-14.

         Lee, Ernest W. Preprimer lessons. Chapter 5 of
         Literacy primers: The Gudschinsky method.

         Prereading. Section 6 of *Notes on literacy, selected
         articles.* Dallas, Texas: Summer Institute of
         Linguistics, 1979.

Central point for discussion
    The need to deal with language awareness as a basis
    for teaching preliterate people to read.

Questions to consider

- Thinking of the Gudschinsky model of a complete literacy program, where should language awareness drills be incorporated?
- In a literacy class, should language awareness drills precede or follow the use of indigenous literature?
- How does Lee's model of reading account for language awareness?
- What features of the language you are studying will require special awareness drills? What kind of drills do you propose?

Testing the Reading Materials Prepared

Reading   Herzog, Dorothy L. A literature workshop, part III. *Notes on Literacy,* 1974, *17,* 17-22.

Jacobs, Suzanne. Vernacular writing for Micronesians. *Notes on Literacy,* 1977, *22,* 1-18.

Herbert, Pat. Utilising existing social structures for literacy programmes. *Notes on Literacy,* 1979, *27,* 10-13.

Central point for discussion

The need to discover the areas of life in which indigenous writing will be satisfying to many in a society, and how that writing can be expanded and improved.

Questions to consider

- What parts of the Herzog questionnaire are feasible for testing in your situation?
- What cultural problems can you foresee in doing such testing or observing?
- What recordkeeping system can you set up that will require the least paperwork, but which will allow you to tabulate data quickly?
- Suppose little interest is shown by villagers in the materials produced in the workshop. Why should you continue looking for people to train as writers?

Funding and Distribution of Materials

Reading   Havelock, Ronald G., and Havelock, Mary C. *Training of change agents.* Ann Arbor, Michigan: University of Michigan Institute for Social Research, 1973.

Sayers, Keith. Marketing principles for SIL, selected excerpts. *Notes on Literacy*, 1975, *18*, 38-39.

Wendell, Margaret M. A literature workshop: Part II. *Notes on Literacy*, 1974, *17*, 6-16.

Wendell, Margaret M. Writer-training workshops, appendix D. *Notes on Literacy*, 1975, *18*, 24-27.

Central point for discussion

How to begin a literacy program so that it quickly becomes financially independent.

Questions to consider

• Havelock and Havelock's treatment of their proposition that "user-initiated change is the most likely to endure" does not specifically mention funding. Why can funding of a literature program, however small, be considered an essential part of user-initiated change?

• How might grants by foundations or other agencies be used to introduce literature into a society without doing harm to the goal of a truly indigenous program of literacy? What pitfalls can be foreseen? How can proper planning and communication forestall problems?

• What literature funding needs do you foresee in the area where you work? How might you go about securing the financial support of the community?

• What is the average annual income in the area where you work? What facts can you cite (other than poor clothing and housing) to describe the economic level? When do people spend money or its equivalent? For what things or events?

• What techniques of distribution need to be emphasized? How do these match norms in your area? What adaptations must be made?

Continuing Indigenous Literacy Program:
Pipe Dream or Possibility?

Reading   Cates, Ann. *Strategies for developing reading acquisition programmes in a face-to-face society.* Unpublished manuscript. Dallas: Summer Institute of Linguistics, 1978.

Dennis, Lynn. Motivation for literacy among the Tolpan. *Notes on Literacy,* 1979, *27,* 1-9.

Central point for discussion

A preliterate society is not likely to turn into a literate society without some planning and help.

Question to consider

- What have you done or what do you plan to do to uncover motivation for reading in the group where you work?
- Do you envision the group with which you work as being able to carry on its own program of literacy and literature? Why or why not?
- What planning have you done toward such a goal?
- What must occur before such a goal can be realized?
- Through what areas or levels or society would you choose to work in order to achieve the goal of a literate society?
- What resources, already at hand, can be tapped? What other resources need to be found?
- When do you expect to bow out, leaving a program that will continue without your help?

Chapter Eleven

Summary

Reading, above all other skills, characterizes any society that seeks to participate in today's world. It has been of serious concern to literacy agencies that there still exist entire societies for whom the nature and process of reading are very mysterious. We have termed these societies "preliterate," for reading does not enter into their lives. In times past, lack of reading skills has not hindered in anyway the full operation of such a society. But those days are gone. The industrialized world spreads into and across the geographical boundaries of the preliterate groups, whose need for literacy is becoming urgent. But for these "forgotten peoples" the full implication of reading still remains a mystery.

The theme throughout this book is that the mystery concerning reading can be more easily and quickly removed by an early introduction of reading material, before major emphasis is made on a widespread program to teach reading skills. However, this material will be useless for showing what reading is all about unless close attention is paid to two basic factors: 1) it must be in the heart language of the people for whom it is intended, and 2) the content must clearly reflect the culture of the people for whom it is intended. The fastest and surest way of obtaining such desirable reading material is to train native speakers of the target language to write their thoughts, experiences, and stories in their own language and in their own indigenous style. These may be written by their own hand or dictated to someone else who can write.

As people see mystery and "foreignness" removed from the printed page, motivation for learning to read increases. Willingness, even eagerness, to incorporate the written message into the life of a society is born. The high risk of lapse into illiteracy, sadly prevalent as a post-literacy campaign effect, is greatly reduced.

Once the step has been taken into literacy in the indigenous language and society, the next step of learning to speak and read the national language is no longer a gigantic leap. If local authors are trained not only to write, but also to duplicate and distribute their work, a preliterate society will soon reach the stage where it can be termed a literate society— one that is ready to move into the larger linguistic and social framework, if it so desires.

Members of the Summer Institute of Linguistics, working in some seven hundred preliterate societies, have been incorporating writer-training projects into many of their programs of linguistic investigation and Scripture translation. The past eight years have seen a marked increase in such projects, a result of the instigation of writer-training workshops in most of the countries where members of the Summer Institute of Linguistics are studying indigenous languages. The first of these workshops was held in Mexico, in 1970, and served as a model for the others. Through many subsequent workshops procedures have been expanded and refined, with the devleopment of many innovative approaches. This book has attempted to bring together both rationale and current procedure for conducting writer-training workshops.

Part One of the book has focused on rationale and basic elements of a writer-training program, regardless of whether the training is done locally and informally or in a formal workshop. Results, advantages, and problems have been discussed.

Part Two presented details of a workshop program for the use of anyone anticipating such responsibility. The details have been compiled from reports submitted by colleagues of the Summer Institute of Linguistics as well as from the author's reports and recollections of workshops held in six countries.

The reader may well ask: Is an ongoing, self-sustaining

program of indigenous literature a realistic goal for a pre-literate society speaking a minority language only recently put into written form? Are not the pressures to move out of the mother tongue and into a major language so strong that it is useless to begin a program of literature production?

In this writer's opinion, it is not important to foretell the final outcome of the language policy of a particular society. It is important that the group be given the option of deciding what language they want to write in. However, how can an option be presented unless the group has seen that the language with which they are most familiar can serve in written form just as well as the major language, though for different purposes and in different circumstances? How else can opportunity for choice be given?

It is the deep conviction of this writer, and of many colleagues in the Literacy Department of the Summer Institute of Linguistics, that each society deserves the right to use its language in written form, and to experience the delight that inevitably accompanies the writing. Our observation that this occurs has made us persist in finding ways to make it possible for many people to experience the same exuberance exhibited by the young Camerounian writer who exclaimed, "There has never, ever been anything written in my language, and *I have made the first book!*"

It is hoped that the discussion on these pages will eventually open the way for many representatives of many pre-literate societies to experience similar exultation of spirit.

Appendix A

Sample Writings

Six examples of original writing are presented, with translations into English either in full or in synopsis. They represent spontaneous, voluntary writing following workshop training.

Unless otherwise indicated, the writings were published in a limited trial edition (25 to 100 copies) by the Summer Institute of Linguistics working in the country named.

Sample 1
   Country: Papua New Guinea
   Language: Usarufa
   Author: Yaaneqo (a young boy from the village of Kaagu in the
           Kaiantu Subdistrict of the Eastern Highlands)

Excerpts from: naaópaqa wátáama
   nopí móra-iyapogoma nommá péráimma pukáiye. pukáitan-
   ama móra-iyapogoma maména naaópaqa utáiye. uta-yáka-
   raiye. aboámá ibiqá yakáiye. anóama ibiqá yakáiye.

Home—News

One boy died while bathing in the river. He died and another boy came and brought him home. He buried him. His father cried. His mother cried.
   waíma abáá kéunanama augáágómá tiyáápi túpukaiye.
   túpukaitaga "u-yau-ya!" tiráune. taáqa óri umá karáitaqa
   ibiqá yakáune. min-áúgáámá moyámma iká-naraae, iká-
   natuwaawana anóama ibiqá yakáiye.

I was looking for rats when a cassowary bit me in the hand. It bit me and I said, "u-yau-ya!" I was very afraid and I cried. Someone stole that cassowary, killed and ate it and its mother (owner) cried.

nokáápake táoma tiyáákama yáqtokaune. yáqtoqmeqa yaayúqnobaqa iramá agamakéqa táoma agamá naráune. nátuweqa Negibípaqa uréqa aaniq-áániqa koma yayúqmeqa iráune. tinima kú-naraune.

From in the night I caught ten frogs. I caught them, built a fire in the woods, cooked the frogs and ate them. After eating them I went to Negibi and pulled up some onions I came. In a tin I cooked and ate them.

Sample 2
    Country: Mexico
    Language: Zapoteco del Istmo
    Author: María Villalobos Villalobos
    The following story is one of four original "fables" by the above-named author.

STIIDXA CHUPA GUBAANA'

Sicari bizaaca lú ti be'te huiini'. Casi bidxí layú biree ziyubi ni go. Nécati biree me ralidxi me bidxaaga me ti mistu gui'xhi', na rabi laame:
—Paraa cheu', be'te bichi.
—Chi yube xiixa guiaba jlaagua'—na me.
—Zanda chi neu naa la?—na mistu gui'xhi rabi laame.
—Zanda pue —na me.
    Para biree iropa came ze came, ziyui' came diidxa'. Na mistu gui'xhi rabi laame:
—Xi jma cului'la'dxu go lo yana gueela'.
De guluuñe huiini me ique me, na me:
—Neca bia' chonna si xandie ne chupa chonna zee. Laga lii ya' —rabi me mistu gui'xhi'.
—Laca cadi stale —na—neca chupa chonna si bere.
Zaqué ziyui' came diidxa dede yendá came ra nuu ti ranchu. Para na mistu gui'xhi rabi laame:
—Rari indaa saa nu, bichi. Idu'ya nu tu jma guiaba ni laa, ne laca rari idxaaga nu para chibi' nu, bichi.
Biree came ze came. Mistu gui'xhi ze luguiá bere. Laame ze me luguiá xandié ne zee. Chaahui chaahui gudxi'ba mistu gui'xhi lu ti yaga ra dxi'ba jma bere. Nécati zidxiña ti binni bi'ni ca bere que ruidu. Biree xpixuaana yoo que bichenda ti paliza xa diaga, ziyaba rilú biete ti zi uxooñe'.
    Dxa be'te laca chicué' chicué' ziyuu xa'na ti le'. Yácati chindá me ra nuu xandié biaaxha ti bi'cu bichá ruaa ñee me, peru gunda biree yaande me ze me. Chiita chiita yendá me ra nuu mistu gui'xhi'. Para na mistu gui'xhi rabi laame:
—Biaba ni lii la? bichi.
—Biaba —na me— cadi cayuuyu la? Dede ma qué ganda saya' tantu dxá ndaane'. Laga lii ya —rabi me laa.

—Laaca —na— dede ndaani ique dxá ni —na ruluí' ná ique ra unaaze palu que, dxá gui.

Zaca biziidi iropa came cadi chi ndana came sti binni.

The Story of Two Thieves

Here's what happened to a little skunk. As it was getting dark he went out to look for something to eat. He had no more than come out of his house when he met a fox who said to him, "Where are you going, friend skunk?"

The skunk said, "I am going to look for something that will fall well on my gizzard."

"Can I go with you?" asked the fox.

"Sure," answered the skunk.

So they both left, talking as they went. The fox asked, "What do you want most to eat tonite?"

The skunk scratched his head a little and said, "Even if I only find around three watermelons and two or three ears of corn. And you, what do you want?" he asked the fox.

"I don't want much either—just two or three chickens."

They went on talking like that until they arrived at a ranch. Then the fox said, "Here we will go our separate ways, friend. We'll see who has the greater landfall, and we'll meet back here to go home."

So they set off. The fox was intent upon finding a chicken. The skunk was looking for watermelons and corn. Stealthily the fox climbed a tree where lots of chickens were roosting. Just as soon as he got near the chickens they made a great deal of commotion. The owner came out and let the fox have it behind the ear with a machete. He quickly slid down the tree and ran off.

The skunk also cautiously went under a fence. He had almost arrived at the watermelons when a dog grabbed hold of his foot, but he was able to escape. Limping, he arrived back where the fox was. The fox said to him, "Did it go well with you, brother?"

"Yes, very well," said the skunk. "Can't you see? I'm so full I can't even walk. And you?"

"I too fared very well; even my head is full," the fox answered pointing to his head which was swollen from the blow.

And that's how it was that both of them learned not to take what belonged to someone else.

Sample 3
    Country: Ghana
    Language: Konkomba
    Author: Gideon Taadimie Jagir
Drawing from his observations and experiences as a nurse-in-training, the author wrote a nine-page booklet entitled *Asibti* (The Hospital) to help village people of his language group understand what to expect if they should go to the hospital for treatment or for surgery. The booklet is divided into four parts: The Out-Patient Department, The Doctor's Consulting Room, Serious Sickness, and Operation.

The following is Mr. Jagir's translation into English of the fourth section, Operation.

I want to tell you how they operate people in hospital. I cannot tell you about all types of operations, but I will tell you how they operate on strangulated hernias.

If someone has a strangulated hernia and they bring him to the hospital, the nurses will put him in a bed . . . . When they finish doing that they shave the private part and put (cloth) soaked in cold water onto the strangulation. After that they will inject him once and he sleeps. By the time he wakes up the strangulation will be gone.

If they will operate on someone, the day before the day of the operation he will not eat food which is heavy for the stomach. That day, early in the morning, they will do an enema . . . . They will use a medicine to (make it) clean clean clean . . . and they put a towel to cover that place.

If they are going to operate on him they will ask him whether he wants it or not. If he says he wants them to, they will operate, if he says he doesn't want it, they won't operate. If he said he wants it, then they put him on the "chain"—it's not a proper chain, it's like a table. Then he will leave and they push him to the operating room. Then they remove him from the chain and put him on the operating table. Then one man is there and he will inject him again, and when he finishes he will be asleep. And when he is asleep, then the doctor will start operating. When they finish operating, they will re-sew it and put on a plaster, and when that is finished they will return him to his room.

There his eyes will open again. After the operation they will give him medicine, and seven days later they will remove the ropes (stitches) which they have sewn. Then it won't be long before he becomes well. When he has finished getting well, the doctor discharges him to go home.

Some people say they kill people when they operate on them. It is not true.

If you are sick and they want to operate on you, let them operate on you. Don't be afraid and try your "luck"—if sickness gets you, bring it to the hospital quickly quickly.

Sample 4
Country: Mexico
Language: Totonaco de Papantla
Author: "Xamanixna" (The Dreamer)

For reasons known best to him, the Totonac author/poet desired to use a pseudonym rather than his full name. In deference to that wish, we continue the practice here, although the man is no longer living.

Eleven of the poems written by "Xamanixna" (sha-ma-neesh-na) are included in the collection. The subjects are as follows:

"I Looked Again for You"
"Why Do You Want to Leave?"
"Love Me!"
"Memories"
"Disgust"
"The Meeting"
"Why Are We Angry?"
"Father, Why Do You Beat Me?"
"Woman"
"I Do Not Love You"

The following is the first verse of "Woman." It tells the thoughts of a young man who loves a beautiful woman. He speaks of her with affection, love, and deep admiration.

PUSCAT

Camaklhtinanti quintachihuin
Nima taxtu ixpulacni quinac'u:
Milakastapu la st'acu lakskoy,
Huix la katum x'anat sala c'achiqu'in,
Que ni la mascaca quilhtamac'u,
Y nac quilatamat siempre lakaskoy.

The following is the first verse of the poem entitled, "Father, Why Do You Beat Me?" They are the words of a young boy who loves his father very much, but the father often hits him. The child pleads that he not be beaten so often, for he is very sensitive to this lack of love.

HUANCHI QUISNOKA?

Tata, huanchi quintancsnok'a?
Aquit cpuhuan acxni quisnok'a,
Xlacata lihua chu quisnok'a,
Y xamakapitzi, ni snun casnoka.
Aquit snun cpaxqu'iyan,
Por eso chi clihuaniyan
Xlacata quilistacni cliniyan,
Y hui ni tamaktak'alhni na nacmaxqu'iyan.

Sample 5
Country: Guatemala
Language: Quiché
Author: Santiago Yac Sam
The following is the first of many poems written by Santiago
Yac Sam, who now teaches writing in workshops held regularly for
teachers and other Quiché speaking people who desire to learn to
write in their own ancient language.

Ri Jun Nima' U Bi' San Juan

Ri nima' ri' jela' c'o chunakaj jun tinimit u bi' Aguacatán re
    Nabjul (Huehuetenango).
Chunkajbal k'ij c'o wi,
Craj jun legua c'o wi che ri tinimit.

Cabixic chi ri kas cäq'uiy wi ulok ri nima'chunakaj ri jun
    tinimit u bi'San Juan.
Tec'uri' coc ulok chuxe' ri juyub,
Cubinbej chuxe' ri ulew.

Tec'un' quel chi ulok chunakaj ri tinimit Aguacatán.
Chuxe' jun juyub ri siblaj chak'ij quel wi ulok, ri puro abaj.
Ri joron sibalaj sak lo'loj quel ulok chuxe' tak ri abaj, Cuban
    jun nimalaj c'wa'.
Tec'ur' cätoxin chbic
    Cuban jun nimalaj nima', cäbec.

The Great River of San Juan

There is a great river near the town which they call Aguacatán
    of Huehuetenango.
It is on the side where the sun rises
About one league away from town.

They say the river is born near a town called San Juan.
It springs from beneath a mountain
And travels many leagues under the earth.

Then it surges out near the town of Aguacatán,
From beneath the mountain of solid rock it rises.

The water comes forth pure and clean from beneath the stones
And makes a great well.
the water overflows,
    And makes a great river.

(Translation by Marilyn Henne and Margaret Wendell.)

Sample 6
    Country: Nigeria
    Language: Engenni
    Author: Mosaic Urugba
    The following are translations (by SIL field linguist Joycelyn
Clevenger) of three poems from *Ogwe Unwoni Ekomu Dyomanu* (A
Collection of Poems) published by the above author.

What Is in One's Own Hand Is the Most Imporant

In this world, what is in one's own hand is what is most important.
What I have is mine.
What you have is yours.
What we have is our own.

For another man cannot be proud of what is in our hands, or of what
is in someone else's hand.

Therefore in this world, let me too have something of my own.

An Engenni Man's Advice

Don't rush through life. Don't hurry.
Rushing cannot help you.
You will be able to paddle your canoe against the current of the
    Orashi River.
Persevere,
And be of good courage like a true Engenni man,
And go on paddling upstream without rushing.

Do not get angry.
Do not judge anyone else or yourself either.
And one day you will reach your landing place,
And then you will be happy, and you will forget about the
    current.

River Orashi

River Orashi, blessings on you for the good way you look
after us.
> You have run your course close to where we live so we
> know you well.
>
> Both adults and children swim and enjoy themselves
> in you.
>
> They also paddle their canoes through you to wherever
> they want to go, and this pleases you.

River Orashi, you have done well in coming here for us.
> You have collected much sand along your banks for
> our use.
>
> You have stored much gravel inside you for our use.
>
> You are full of water with which you cool our bodies.
>
> You have many fish and other creatures in you with
> which you feed us.

River Orashi, you flow south, you never flow north.
> Sometimes you rise from the place where you are and
> come and flood the ground near you.
>
> You make the ground wet so that food will grow for us.
>
> When you flood your banks like this, you swallow up all
> the rubbish on the ground and carry it back to
> where you came from,
>
> And the ground is left clean.

River Orashi, honour be to you!
> But even greater honour be to God who made you as
> you are!

Appendix B

Sample Schedules and Other Helps

The following sample items are included in Appendix B.

Sample 1. Schedule for Three-Day Workshop

Sample 2. Schedule for One-Week Workshop

Sample 3. Schedule for Three-Week Workshop

Sample 4. Background Information Questionnaire

Sample 5. Certificate in English

Sample 6. Certificate in Spanish

Sample 7. Closing Program

Sample 1. Schedule for Three-Day Workshop
(Based on workshop directed by Frances Jackson, held for Choctaw teacher aides in Mississippi, March 1978)

	Day 1	Day 2	Day 3
8:00	Opening ceremony.	Discussion: Difficulties encountered yesterday.	Discussion: Difficulties encountered yesterday.
8:30	Class: Literature currently available, stages of literature, culture preservation, responsibility toward community. Workshop goal: publish collection of articles.	Class: Editing, principles of.	Choose order of articles for workshop publication and mimeograph.
9:00	Writing: Discussion, stimulation for writing. Writing begun.	Practice Editing: 1. Self-editing on Ex. 1. 2. Read aloud. 3. Group editing. 4. Rewrite and turn in for typing.	
11:00	Class: Planning a workshop publication. Choosing a topic for article or story.	Writing, Ex. 3 Write and illustrate story for children (something from your own childhood).	
12:00	Lunch	Lunch	Lunch
12:45	Writing, Ex. 1 1. Article for workshop publication. 2. Record article/story on tape, listen, write story. Listen again, revise story. Repeat if desired.	Editing of Ex. 2 Rewrite for publication, turn in to typists (stencils).	Collate workshop publication. Discussion: A Choctaw section in local newspaper?
2:00	Stimulus: Take short walk. Jot down ideas for future articles.	Edit Ex. 3 (Break - 15 min.)	2:30 Closing ceremony.
3:00-4:30	Writing, Ex. 2 Story or article based on stimulus.	Rewrite Ex. 3 for publication, turn in to typists (stencils).	

Sample 2. Schedule for One-Week Workshop
(Based on workshop directed by Marilyn Henne, held in Guatemala, November 1975 for Quiche & Cakchiquel writers)

	Monday	Tuesday	Wednesday	Thursday	Friday	Saturday
8:00		Class: How to write vividly.	Class: How to develop and expand a theme.	Writing: Finish newspapers.	Writing: Finish skits.	Full session: Review of course, suggestion for future courses.
9:00	Registration of trainees.	Practice writing.	Class: What is of interest to home community.		Read skits aloud.	
10:00	Meeting of officers of Mayan Writers Association.	Coffee break				
10:30		Class: How to write a personal experience.	Writing: A theme useful for community, family, etc.	Newspapers presented in contest.	Lecture: The value of the Mayan Culture (visiting professor).	Closing ceremony.
12:00	Lunch					
1:30	Opening Ceremony.	Free				
2:30	Class: Orthography.	Illustrating the pamphlets.	Class: Newspapers	Class: Writing letters and petitions.	Class: How to edit/revise your article.	
3:30	Refreshment Break					

Time					
4:00 5:30	Orthography continued.	Drawing pictures.	Small groups: Plan a newspaper and begin articles.	Class: Writing skits for radio, school, church, etc.	Class: How to use the dictionary.
6:00	Supper				
7:00	Social: Cakchiquel group in charge.	Discussion led by Association officer.	Round table discussion: Cakchiquel group in charge.	Mayan Writers Association meeting.	Cultural program and movie: Quiche group in charge.

Sample 3. Schedule for Three-Week Workshop
(Based on workshop directed by Frances Wood held in Nepal, July 1974)

	Week One	Monday	Tuesday	Wednesday	Thursday	Friday
For Field Linguists	Lecture I		Literacy and cultural implications.	Prereading activities.		
	Lecture II		Total literacy program.	Postprimer materials.		
For Writer-Trainees	Class discussion	Registration, housing, etc.	Introduction to workshop goals.	Communication by storytelling: kinds, ways, personnel, etc.	Individual consultations: problems, clarification of purpose of workshop, etc.	Different types of literature.
	Practice Lab	Opening ceremony.	Getting started.	Share writings of yesterday.		Share reports of visit to cookie factory. Discuss ways to improve writing.
	Writing assignment	Social time.	First trip to capital.	List kind of books desired in own language.	Write up visit to cookie factory.	Rewrite report. Prepare translation into Nepali.
	Art assignment		Draw a picture to illustrate writing.	Practice drawing, compare village art styles.		Illustrate report.
	Excursion			Visit to cookie factory.		

Sample 3 (continued)

	Week Two	Monday	Tuesday	Wednesday	Thursday	Friday
For Field Linguists	Lecture I		Teaching of arithmetic.	Style: oral vs. written.		Worksheets for related languages. Editing.
	Lecture II		Introduction to creative writing: style, types, etc.	Cultural learning styles. Cultural "drives."		Newspapers. Readability. Share English translation of reports.
For Writer-Trainees	Class discussion	Types of literature (continued).		Styles: Plain vs. eloquent; informal vs. formal.	Individual consultations: problems, plans, immediate and long range.	Editing.
	Practice lab	Read the improved reports.		Discuss trip. Share written reports.		Share reports of Gorkhapatra, edit. Plan illustration.
	Writing assignment	Type up report and its translation for checking.	Write up report of trip to King's Forest.	1. Write "trip to bazaar" for children; for village elders. 2. Work on King's Forest report.	Write report of Gorkhapatra experience.	Rewrite Gorkhapatra report. Review previously written notes.
	Art assignment		Illustrate the report (1 picture).			Practice drawing over weekend: trees, animals, people, houses.
	Excursion	Leave for King's Forest 3:00 p.m.		Leave for Gorkhapatra 5:30 p.m.		

Sample 3 (continued)

	Week Three	Monday	Tuesday	Wednesday	Thursday	Friday
For Field Linguists	Lecture I	Pedagogy.				
	Lecture II	Factors involved in planning a literacy program.				
For Writer-Trainees	Class discussion	Village newspapers. Art instruction by Nepali artist.	Plan content of workshop newspaper.	Work on newspaper articles.	Prepare stencils for newspaper and duplicate.	Collate newspaper.
	Practice lab	Read remaining stories for group reaction.	Share humorous stories, edit.			Practice for closing ceremony.
	Writing assignment	Write story to make people laugh.	Rewrite humorous story.	Make sure all articles are translated into Nepali; complete any unfinished work.		
	Art assignment	Practice drawing according to Nepali artist's instructions.	Group: plan layout of newspaper.			
	Excursion			Committee chooses stories to be read for closing ceremony.		Closing ceremony.

Sample 4. *Background Information Questionnaire*
(To be filled in by Field Linguist and given to Workshop Director)
1. Name of trainee _____
2. Name of language _____
3. Location of language area _____
4. What major language does she/he speak? _____
5. Educational background _____

6. Temperament (e.g., introvert, extrovert, etc.) _____

7. Normal occupation _____

8. Does he/she type? _____ If not, have you a typewriter that can be
   loaned? _____
9. Has he/she spent much time outside the village? _____

10. Has the trainee done any writing previously? _____ If so, list titles or
    topics on reverse side.
11. Have you seen evidence of artistic ability? _____ If so, in what way? _
12. Has the orthography of the trainee's language been tested satisfactorily?
    Please describe _____
    _____
    _____

Sample 5. Sample Certificate in English

CERTIFICATE

This is to certify that _____ has
participated in a Workshop for the purpose of producing reading materials
in the _____ language, held in _____ from (beginning
date) to (ending date). She/he has attended _____ sessions.

	_____
GOLD	Director, Summer Institute of Linguistics
	_____
SEAL	Workshop Director
	_____
(ribbons	Workshop Assistant
in	_____
national	Workshop Assistant
colors)	

Sample Schedules

Sample 6. Sample Certificate in Spanish

GOLD

C E R T I F I C A D O   SEAL (ribbons
in
national
El Instituto Lingüístico de Verano   colors)
extiende el presente Certificado el día _____ de _____
de _____, y en el cual se hace constar que el (la) Senor/Senorita

ha participado como alumno (a) en el Curso de Capacitación para la Prepara-
ción de Materiales de Lectura en la Lengua _____

MAESTROS:

Lugar
Directores:

_____

_____   _____

_____

Sample 7. Closing Program
(Based on "Programa de Clausura" used in a Colombia workshop, directed by
Frances Jackson, October 1979)

1. Invocation
2. Introductions
3. Welcome to distinguished guests
4. National hymn
5. Summary of the course (given by a writer-trainee)
6. Reading of original works by their authors (translated into national
language)
7. Demonstration of touch-typing
8. Musical number
9. Address by visiting official
10. Presentation of certificates
11. Refreshments and exhibition of writings completed and in progress

Appendix C

How to Construct a Silk-Screen Mimeograph

Adapted from John Tomlinson, VITA

Volunteer, Rochester, New York as presented

in VITA Handbook

SILK-SCREEN PRINTING
Silk-screen printing is a simple, inexpensive method of producing multiple copies of attractive visual aids, posters, and other materials, including typewritten pages. A "squeegee" forces very thick paint (or ink) through those parts of the silk-screen which are exposed by the stencil onto paper placed underneath the screen.

MATERIALS NEEDED
2 hinges, about 1″ x 3″ (preferably with removable pins)
wing or regular nuts
8″ or 9″ squeegee
trigger support (see Figure 2)
wood for frame, 6 ft. of 2″ x 3/4″
3/4″ plywood approximately 20″ x 24″ (or any board that size), must be very smooth—preferably painted or varnished
silk or other sheer cloth (nylon works fine) 25″ x 18″
1 box thumbtacks
mimeograph ink

INSTRUCTIONS FOR BUILDING
1. Build the frame (see Figures 1 and 2), using 3/4″ x 2″ wood. The frame should have an inner dimension 15″ x 10″ if used with regular mimeograph stencils, but could be made larger if needed. Make sure the corners are square, using a half-lap joint to avoid any shifting. Joint may be glued, but dowels or screws in addition will give greater strength and prevent warping in humid climates. Be sure the frame lies flat against the baseboard. A few coats of spar type varnish will make both frame and base longer lasting and less apt to warp or mold.

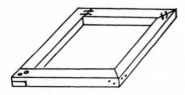

FIGURE 1. MAKING THE FRAME OF THE SILK-SCREEN. DIFFERENT JOINT CONSTRUCTIONS ARE SHOWN AT EACH CORNER; ANY ONE OF THESE MAY BE USED FOR THE JOINTS OF THE FRAME.

2. Stretch the silk very tighty over the *underside* of the frame, using tacks every inch or so, and making sure that the threads of the silk run parallel to the edges of the frame. Pull the silk over the outside bottom edges and up onto the top, tightening the four corners squarely first and then lining up the sides and tightening them. Since the silk is inclined to sag again after the first using, you may want to use a couple of narrow strips of wood to enable you to retighten one end and side (see Figure 2).

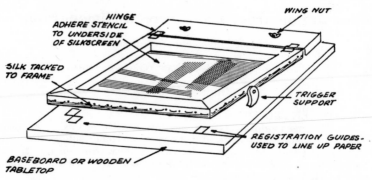

HINGE
ADHERE STENCIL TO UNDERSIDE OF SILKSCREEN
WING NUT
SILK TACKED TO FRAME
TRIGGER SUPPORT
REGISTRATION GUIDES. USED TO LINE UP PAPER
BASEBOARD OR WOODEN TABLETOP

FIGURE 2. BOLT THE HINGED END OF THE FRAME TO A FLAT BASEBOARD OR WOODEN TABLE TOP.

3. The squeegee can be bought at an art supply store, a department store, or a hardware store. Or, if none are available, it can be made according to Figure 3.

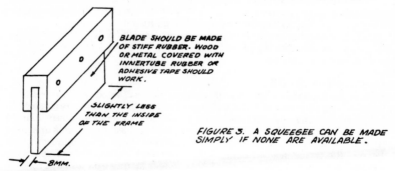

BLADE SHOULD BE MADE OF STIFF RUBBER. WOOD OR METAL COVERED WITH INNERTUBE RUBBER OR ADHESIVE TAPE SHOULD WORK.

SLIGHTLY LESS THAN THE INSIDE OF THE FRAME

8MM.

FIGURE 3. A SQUEEGEE CAN BE MADE SIMPLY IF NONE ARE AVAILABLE.

INSTRUCTIONS FOR PRINTING

1. Any regular mimeograph stencil may be used. Stencil may be cut in the usual way on a typewriter, and drawings may be made with a regular mimeograph stylus or with a ballpoint pen that no longer writes. If you wish to use the sides of the stencil as top and bottom in order to make your books, it is possible to cut the stencil in half for insertion into the typewriter if the carriage is too short. It is not necessary to glue them back together. By positioning them with about 1/4" overlap, both pieces will remain adhered to the silk when the ink is applied. (Note: The cardboard tab can be torn off once the stencil is cut, as it is not necessary for using the stencil with the silk-screen and the tab just gets in the way.)

2. a. Place a piece of paper the size to be printed directly under the silk-screen to be used as a guide for the placement of the stencil.

b. Lay the typed stencil directly on this piece of paper, positioning it for the centering of the printed page, etc. The stencil should be right side up (so it can be read).

c. Now lower the silk frame into position, and squeeze a line of ink about the thickness of your little finger across the top of the silk, the width of the paper to be printed (Figure 4).

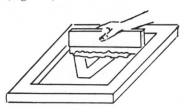

FIGURE 4. THE SQUEEGEE IS USED TO DRAW THE THICK PAINT ACROSS THE SILK SCREEN.

d. With the squeegee, spread the ink evenly over the area with several firm strokes, making sure the ink penetrates the silk sufficiently to make a strong, readable impression on the paper. This will also help the stencil adhere to the silk. If it does not do so, you may need to add a small amount of ink until it does. Test with several pieces of scratch paper until you are satisfied with darkness of printing, centering on the paper, etc.

e. Once you have a clear copy, you are ready to begin printing. Place a stack of 10-20 sheets of paper on the guidelines on the base. Lower the silk-screen and with one firm, steady stroke pull the squeegee to the bottom of the frame. Lift the screen and remove the print, placing a "slip sheet" on top of it. Proceed to the next sheet, always pulling the sequeegee toward you. (Note: It may be necessary occasionally to pull the squeegee in the opposite direction in order to remove the ink that has accumulated.) Continue in this manner until the total number of pages have been run. Allow sufficient time for the ink to dry (2-24 hours, depending on the humidity) before printing the other side of the paper.